Images of Modern America

LGBTQ
CINCINNATI

Images of Modern America

LGBTQ CINCINNATI

KEN SCHNECK
FOREWORD BY JIM OBERGEFELL

ARCADIA
PUBLISHING

Copyright © 2020 by Ken Schneck
ISBN 978-1-4671-0511-8

Published by Arcadia Publishing
Charleston, South Carolina

Printed in the United States of America

Library of Congress Control Number: 2019954293

For all general information, please contact Arcadia Publishing:
Telephone 843-853-2070
Fax 843-853-0044
E-mail sales@arcadiapublishing.com
For customer service and orders:
Toll-Free 1-888-313-2665

Visit us on the Internet at www.arcadiapublishing.com

Dedicated to the LGBTQ community of Cincinnati, who fought, shouted, wrote, marched, and celebrated to create what we have today

CONTENTS

Foreword   6

Acknowledgments   7

Introduction   8

1.   We Connect: Groups, Activities, and Spaces   11

2.   We Gather: Spaces and Events   29

3.   We Communicate: Media   47

4.   We Organize: Activism and Issues   61

5.   We March: Pride Celebrations   79

About the Ohio Lesbian Archives   95

FOREWORD

"I think the actions of the City of Cincinnati, over the last decade or so, indicate that the city is very sympathetic to the idea that Ohio should be a place where same-sex marriage is permitted."

Cincinnati city attorney Aaron Herzig spoke these words on July 22, 2013, during a hearing in the US District Court for the Southern District of Ohio in Downtown Cincinnati. I was in that courtroom, seated on one side with civil rights attorney Al Gerhardstein and his team. Herzog and Bridget Coontz, an assistant attorney general for the State of Ohio, sat on the other side of the courtroom. My husband, John, was not in the courtroom because he was bedridden due to ALS, also known as Lou Gehrig's Disease.

John and I had sued the State of Ohio and the City of Cincinnati to demand recognition of our lawful Maryland marriage. We knew that John was dying of ALS, and we wanted his death certificate to accurately reflect that he died a lawfully married man and that I was his surviving spouse. This was our day in federal court.

With his words, Herzog made it clear that Cincinnati had changed drastically from the extremely conservative place it was when I arrived in 1984 to attend the University of Cincinnati. I remember feeling stunned on this July 2013 day once I realized that Cincinnati's leaders were saying that they wanted nothing to do with this lawsuit because they believed our marriage deserved to be treated just like any other.

How could this be? This is the city whose residents amended the city charter to prohibit any laws or policies that would protect the LGBTQ+ community. This is the city whose Contemporary Arts Center director was prosecuted for obscenity after exhibiting a collection of photographs by Robert Mapplethorpe. This is where undercover city police would ask gay men, "What are you into?" in park bathrooms and then arrest them. This was a place where, from my perspective, people survived by fitting in, by not being too different, and by fulfilling the just be "normal" expectations of their neighbors.

Yet here was city leadership stating in federal court that not only did they believe it was okay for two men to get married but also that they respected that relationship and wanted to protect it just like any other. Change really had come to Cincinnati, the same city once dubbed "the town without pity" by *Esquire* magazine and "puritanical" by writer John Updike.

Less than two years after that hearing, the Supreme Court of the United States brought marriage equality to the nation with their decision in *Obergefell v. Hodges*. During the course of our case, I was constantly struck by the pride I saw on the faces of my fellow Cincinnatians, how thrilled they were that the story of the named plaintiff in this landmark case had taken place in their city. I saw pride in the changes that had occurred in Cincinnati, from personal changes in attitudes to public changes in policies and laws.

After decades of hard work by countless members of the LGBTQ+ community and our allies, Cincinnati is now a city where one's sexual orientation or gender identity is respected and protected. The city that had once banned protections for the LGBTQ+ community became the second city in the nation to ban conversion therapy. The city that many considered to be the most gay-unfriendly city in the nation became the city known as a welcoming and supportive place for the LGBTQ+ community.

The people of Cincinnati are proud of the progress that has occurred in "the Queen of the West," a pride publicly proclaimed by a street sign in the heart of Over-the-Rhine honoring two gay men: John Arthur and Jim Obergefell Way. Positive change does happen, and I'm forever grateful to the brave souls who paved the way and helped create a city that would refuse to discriminate against someone because of the person they loved.

—Jim Obergefell

ACKNOWLEDGMENTS

I am extraordinarily nervous that I am going to inadvertently leave a name off of this page. So, I will endeavor to express my thanks chronologically in the order in which I met people in the hopes that I do not miss someone.

Cheryl Eagleson, you set the tone. You told me what my experience was going to be like putting this book together, and holy heck, it was exactly like that. You are my radio hero.

Scott Knox, you immediately explained some of the legal pieces and sent me in so many fruitful directions. Thank you.

Michael Chanak Jr., you supported me every step of this journey. You are a veritable fount of information and lore, but you also helped right my ship when I got discouraged during some choppy waters. I am supremely appreciative.

Phebe Beiser, I cannot even wrap my mind around the invaluable service you have created and maintained with the Ohio Lesbian Archives. You are preserving our stories, our history, and our very lives, and there's no amount of gratitude that would be adequate to write here.

Ron Clemons, your skill at capturing our LGBTQ history is only matched by your generosity of time and spirit.

David Wolff, you not only provided me with crucial photographs, but you even went out and took some extras for me. Now that is above and beyond service.

Terry Payne, you were my knowledge repository for all things Article XII, the most complex part of Cincy's LGBTQ history for me to understand. You lived the fight, you dedicated your energy to the fight, and you helped win the fight.

JAC Stringer, I know getting me images was an absolute chore, but this book would be less than what it is without them. I thank you.

Jeff Bixby, I now know the way to your house by heart. You opened your home and your memories to me, and I am so grateful. You are the educator I aspire to be.

Jim Obergefell, I still cannot believe you said yes to writing a foreword. You are an LGBTQ icon, and I am honored to have your name on this work.

He does not even know it, but Brian DeWitt again came to my rescue as he did for the *LGBTQ Cleveland* and *LGBTQ Columbus* editions: granting access to old issues of *Gay People's Chronicle* for context, which was my go-to resource for what went down on any given date.

Thanks to everyone over at Arcadia Publishing for this opportunity to capture these moments in print, especially Caroline Anderson, who trusts me enough to let me pop up around deadline time with a book in hand.

There were easily 30 to 40 other LGBTQ and ally heroes in Cincinnati who immediately responded when I cried out, "Help!" or "Is this right?!" They are board chairs, historians, nonprofit leaders, and change-makers. Though they cannot all be named, they are present in the images and words throughout the book.

And finally, to the wonderful LGBTQ community in Cincinnati: you may not see your face in a picture. You may not see your name in print. But trust me, you are most definitely in this book. This is a village. And I am proud to live beside you.

Special Reference must be given for the following photographers. Please support them:

- Jason Bechtel—flickr.com/photos/jasephotos
- Doug Cooper Spencer—www.dougcooperspencer.com
- JAC Stringer—midwestgenderqueer.com
- Ty Wesselkamper—tywessphotography.com

INTRODUCTION

We do have people who are individuals. Nobody makes your decisions, and you don't take anybody's word as gospel, or take a position just because it's politically correct. Of course, there are plenty of people who criticize us for having our own opinions.

—Barron Wilson, longtime member of Cincinnati's Gay Community
To the Root(s), Vol. 1, No. 1, Summer 1988

I drove to Cincinnati for the first time with far too much confidence. Having completed the Cleveland and Columbus editions of these LGBTQ history books both within the past 13 months, I went to the Queen City—a gay-adjacent moniker that never ceases to make me smile—wholly unconcerned about the process of collecting images and stories from its residents.

I knew Cincinnati did not have an LGBTQ center or LGBTQ collections in the local museums as their sister cities have, but that would not be a problem. I knew Cincinnati had some sort of history with an Issue 3 or an Article 12 or some other piece of numbered legislation, but that would be easy for me to grasp. And I knew that I did not have any real connections in Cincinnati, but they would doubtlessly welcome me with open arms. I figured I would speed through this last of the big "C" cities and complete my gay Ohio city *Lord of the Rings* trilogy in no time at all.

I was wrong.

My first stop in my Cincinnati journey was at the house of Cheryl Eagleson: for years, the driving force behind Alternating Currents, the second longest-running LGBTQ radio show in the United States. To get a general feel for the project ahead, I began by asking her how she would describe LGBTQ history in Cincinnati.

"We had to had to go through we did by doing it ourselves," she responded without missing a beat.

At the end of our hour together, having sifted through her photographs and memories, she saw my eyes start to widen as she was tossing so many names into the space between us. These were not the names of organizations or state representatives or national figures but were instead the names of a seemingly endless list of specific people from Cincinnati who stepped up in some way or another.

"I can't say this enough: we had to do it ourselves," she said one more time before I left.

Over the 10 months that I spent gathering images, I found that no truer words have ever been spoken. Within a few days of reaching out to people, it became clear that LGBTQ Cincinnati is a community of individuals. They are passionate, driven, and caring, and they do things their own way. They told me over and over again that Cincinnati is decidedly not Cleveland or Columbus: it is a bit more conservative, it is a bit slower to accept change, it is a bit stubborn until you can convince the city otherwise. But when Cincinnati supports you, they told me, the city really stands behind you.

The LGBTQ community has seen that love over the years throughout a rich and decidedly queer Cincinnati history. In the 1920s, patrons could visit the Green Door, where tokens could be bought to buy drinks or time with other men. The Greenwich Tavern, opened in 1936, was well known as a safe place for gay people to congregate. The 1940s saw the opening of the Keyhole at the Gibson Hotel, the Horseshow Bar, Jim's on Eastern Avenue, Jacob's, and Club Melody.

In the 1960s, the Personal Rights Organization was formed, which put out the first gay publication called *PRO*. Then in 1972, the Cincinnati Gay Community group was formed to fight discrimination following a police raid at the Chaperone Club. This group was responsible for organizing the first Cincinnati Pride celebration in 1973, a year before Cleveland's first Pride and almost a decade before Columbus got started.

So much progress followed over the next 20 years: LGBTQ establishments opened, media coverage of LGBTQ rights exploded, and public officials began increasingly recognizing the presence and contributions of LGBTQ people living in Cincinnati.

And then 1993 hit.

What started out as a joyous celebration when the Cincinnati City Council passed an LGBTQ-inclusive nondiscrimination ordinance in 1992 quickly dissipated as opposition began to foment. As a result of this vociferous dissent, the landslide passing of Issue 3 in 1993 led to the creation of Article XII in the charter, making Cincinnati the only city in the country to enshrine language within their governing documents that specifically prohibited LGBTQ individuals from achieving full equality. Rights were not just *repealed* as they were in other cities. Rights were *prohibited*.

The period between 1993 and 2004 was referenced over and over again by every single person with whom I spoke in preparing this book. Every time that specter was raised, it was almost as if you could feel the air delating from a balloon. They explained to me that during that time, activism faltered, organizations struggled to maintain their existence, fundraising dropped, and even full Pride celebrations disappeared for a few years.

And as a community of individuals, it was those individuals in Cincinnati who really felt it. To be a resident of a city that so overwhelmingly voted against your very identity was no less than demoralizing. LGBTQ people needed time to recover from this stunning body blow.

But recover they did.

The efforts leading up to the repeal of Article XII in 2004 are no less than inspiring. In a year when even the state of Ohio banned same-sex marriage, the LGBTQ community in Cincinnati pulled off the only pro-gay ballot initiative in the entire country. Yes, they did it as part of several organizations, but they also did it as individuals: hitting the streets and knocking on doors to have tens of thousands of one-on-one conversations with voters to explain how Article XII affected them as humans. The voters listened, changed course, and Article XII was voted out of Cincinnati's life.

Fast forward to the present day, and you have Cincinnati receiving a perfect score on the Human Rights Campaign's Municipal Equality Index. Sure, Cleveland and Columbus also received the same score, but for Cincinnati, it just feels more special. This rating represents a staggering turnaround in a relatively short amount of time in Cincinnati's history, a numerical representation of a city that struggled mightily with LGBTQ equality and emerged championing their LGBTQ siblings.

These pages are filled to the brim with those LGBTQ citizens of Cincinnati and their triumphs, their setbacks, and their dogged determination to have their voices heard. They did indeed do it themselves, and they created a community in the doing: a community of individuals.

One

WE CONNECT

GROUPS, ACTIVITIES, AND SPACES

From GLUE to MUSE, from AVOC to GCGLC, there has never been a shortage of groups and organizations providing the LGBTQ community an opportunity to come together around common (and sometimes, very specific) interests and plan myriad activities to channel their unique and passionate energy. (Michael Chanak Jr.)

Early in 1970, a group of young, black gay men sat around talking, drinking, and discussing various issues, including the lack of black male social clubs in the Greater Cincinnati area. As a result, the Pacesetters Social Club was formed. Later in the 1970s, a sister chapter was formed in St. Louis. A signature project of the club was to host a Labor of Love weekend, during which members invited out-of-town guests to a full weekend of activities. Both clubs have since been disbanded—Cincinnati's in 1984 and St. Louis's in 1987—but members from both clubs remain friends to this day and continue to visit between the two cities. (Both, Doug Cooper Spencer.)

Created in the late 1970s, the Greater Cincinnati Gay Coalition was formed as an umbrella organization for all of the different LGBTQ groups in Cincinnati to come together and be on the same page. They originally met in the undercroft of the Church of Our Saviour and then moved to All Saints Chapel in 1984, the same year the group's name was changed to Greater Cincinnati Gay and Lesbian Coalition (GCGLC). The roster for the monthly meetings looked like an alphabet soup (ASC, DC, GCSA, LSSG, GLCS, and many, many more). People would go around the room and share what they were doing, create a calendar of events, and coordinate dates so that the groups were supporting each other's efforts. GCGLC was also the group responsible for producing Pride, a true representation of Cincinnati's LGBTQ community with so many groups pitching in to make the event happen. (Both, Jeff Bixby.)

Stonewall Cincinnati was first established in 1982 with the mission of ending discrimination against all people, especially those who faced discrimination based on sexual orientation. The organization stood at the center of so much of the LGBTQ human rights work that has taken place in the Queen City: conducting voter registration, coordinating educational newsletters, hosting their annual dinners, and generally endeavoring to raise up the voices and equality of the LGBTQ community in the city through networking, lobbying, protesting, and organizing. Stonewall was instrumental in leading the efforts in 1992 to pass the Human Rights Ordinance by the Cincinnati City Council. When Issue 3 passed the following year, so much of the LGBTQ citizenry was demoralized, and donations to Stonewall Cincinnati dropped precipitously. In 2001, the organization had to change to an all-volunteer model, no longer able to staff an executive director. Ultimately, the organization met its demise during the fight against Article XII, unable to be the exact champion that the LGBTQ community needed and wanted at that time. (Both, Ron Clemons.)

MUSE, Cincinnati's women's choir, was formed in 1984 by Catherine Roma, a doctoral student in choral conducting at the University of Cincinnati, who wanted to assemble a group to perform works written specifically for women's voices. MUSE made her debut on International Women's Day in 1984 within six weeks of her first rehearsal. By 1985, they appointed Ruth Rowan as signer for the hearing-impaired, serving as interpreter extraordinaire for over 30 years. Performances throughout the decades have included appearances at the Sister Singers Festival, the New Spirituals Project Concerts, GALA International Choral Festivals, and a full slate of concerts in and around the Cincinnati area. Today, MUSE continues to be guided by her original vision of a choral community of feminist women creating a more peaceful and just world through song. (Above, MUSE; below, Philip Groshong.)

AVOC NEWSLETTER

A.I.D.S VOLUNTEERS OF CINCINNATI, INC.
P.O. BOX 19009
CINCINNATI, OHIO 45219

FEBRUARY 19, 1987

AVOC President Reports
by Walter Sherman

New Board Members

Five new members have been elected to the Board of Trustees of AIDS Volunteers of Cincinnati as replacements to members who have resigned.

Tom Zeitz was elected to fill a 1 year term. Tom's principal work for AVOC is to answer calls to the 421-AIDS number which AVOC maintains. Tom answers questions and refers calls when necessary, and will be our liaison to the Northern Kentucky AIDS Task Force. Bob Bastian was elected to a 1 year term and has assumed supervision of the assignment of buddies to AIDS patients and of all volunteer activities and placements. Warren Liang replaces Michael Mavroidis on the Board. Warren is a psychiatrist at University Hospital and works with the AIDS-Related Disorders Clinic there. He will be our medical link to the hospitals and will be writing articles to update us and readers of the Gaybeat on recent developments in AIDS research. Lynn Teisman comes on board with a background in nursing, public relations and grant writing -- necessary work for AVOC as we begin to expand our activities and distribution of funds. And Bob Brockman joins us as the chair of fundraising. Bob and his committee are busy preparing a calendar of events and they will be coordinating all benefits for AVOC as well as our own events.

According to the by-laws, vacant Board positions may be filled by the Board. Total membership on the Board is now 10 persons, by vote at the last annual meeting. Continuing Board members are Walter Sherman, Pat Herrmann, Gloria Buckholz, Robb Martin and Ray Fulwider.

Annual Meeting April 29

The annual meeting for AIDS Volunteers of Cincinnati will take place at St. John's Unitarian/Universalist Church on Resor Avenue in Clifton at 7:30 pm on Wednesday, April 29. Nominations and elections for 5 seats on the Board of Trustees will take place, expenditures and income for 1986 will be presented, by-

laws will be reviewed, and a program (yet to be announced) follows. The meeting will adjourn by 9:00.

Board members "retreat" to consider '87 plans

Board members spent the 3rd Saturday of January in a day-long retreat to plan and organize for 1987. Considering the number of new Board members, the executive council thought it mandatory to bring them "on board," review and critique our work this past year, and work to expand our efforts in 1987. The following ideas, plans and revisions resulted from discussions at the retreat:

--guidelines and contracts for those groups, individuals or institutions agreeing to host benefits for AVOC.

--establishing a monthly 3-hour workshop orientation for persons interested in learning more about AIDS; which will also serve as the requisite training for other AVOC volunteer programs.

--choice of an office location and training/meeting site by the annual meeting.

--development of an intake procedure and policies for use in distributing funds for patient assistance.

--revision of the membership/volunteer form.

--expansion of the existing "buddy" program.

--establishing a trained speakers bureau.

--printing or purchasing more brochures to target audiences

--expanding existing educational and prevention efforts in schools and heterosexual community.

--providing more medical updates for members of AVOC and the community.

--preparing volunteers to staff the AIDS home and our telephone switchboard.

See **President**, page 2

Buddies Program

We would like to welcome the new Buddies Volunteers who completed our 10 week training class in December. Their enthusiasm and willingness to serve the community is an inspiration to all.

Should you know anyone who could use a helping hand, be it a ride to the hospital, a support system or financial aid, give us a call.

The Buddies meet on the 3rd Thursday at 7:30 pm. For more information regarding the Buddies Program, call 421-AIDS.

Congratulations to Rucker & Rhodes; Thanks to Gaybeat

The Board of AVOC extends congratulations to Ronn Rucker and Virginia Rhodes on their selection as Man and Woman of the Year by Gaybeat. Rucker, of the Cincinnati Health Department, has worked vocally to encourage testing for exposure to the AIDS virus and has worked closely with AVOC in its buddy training program. Rhodes, a member of the Cincinnati Public School Board, was instrumental in the adoption of an anti-discrimination statement for teachers or students with AIDS.

Both were honored on January 15 at a cocktail party given by Gaybeat to benefit AVOC's Stop AIDS Cincinnati.

Clothing Bank

AVOC is pleased to announce we have started a clothing bank. AIDS patients lose weight with their illness, and we would like to assist you with many different sizes and varieties of clothing. If you have any clothes you would care to donate, or if you're in need of different sizes due to loss of weight, feel free to call 421-AIDS.

If you need help -- call
421-AIDS

With the onslaught of HIV and AIDS, the citizens of Cincinnati banded together in multiple different ways to both care for their siblings and advocate for changes in society to address the epidemic. Some of the more notable organizations were AIDS Volunteers of Cincinnati (AVOC), STOP AIDS Cincinnati, and Caracole. These organizations have provided testing, educational offerings, social opportunities, resources (such as clothing, housing, and help with medications), and activism. There were also the informal gatherings in the hallways of Holmes Hospital, inside and outside of the AIDS unit, where card games were played in the lobby, laughter was shared, tears were shed, and relationships were formed during just the most impossible of circumstances. (Left, Ohio Lesbian Archives; below, Ron Clemons.)

The Imperial Sovereign Queen City Court of the Buckeye Empire Inc., All of Ohio (ISQCCBE) was born out of the Midwestern bowling league in the early 1980s, taking root in Cincinnati when Miss Buffy was named Imperial Crown Princess in 1988. ISQCCBE now stands as an incorporated nonprofit organization that seeks to support the financial needs of the LGBTQ community through fundraising events, including their popular pageants and Imperial Crown Prince/Princess Ball. The Court's Community News shared ISQCCBE happenings, upcoming events, and awards. The newsletter also included tips on protocol, including "the importance of saying thank you," how to "demonstrate your class, not your crass," and how to appropriately display respect (including "Did you know that it is considered proper to let your reigning monarchs tip or approach a performer first?" and "If a bottle appears out of a purse, protocol dictates that you join in the festivities when the bottle comes your way"). (Both, Jeff Bixby.)

Your Connection to the I.S.Q.C.C.B.E., Inc., All of Ohio, Cincinnati, OH

The Court's Community News

December 1996

Volume 5

Sending An Angel

New Board Members Elected

An angel is, by definition, a messenger sent to convey a unique insight. The holiday greeting cards we send to those we love, also convey a special message of hope for peace and joy. This year, combine the two with our divine "Angels Among Us" greeting cards for this wonderful season. Let those who love you know that you care about the quality of the lives of others for whom words like "Joy" and "Peace" would ring hollow were it not for caring organizations like Aids Volunteers of Cincinnati, and the giving, generous spirit of members of the court and the community at large.

So, be an angel. Pick up the phone and call Dan or Jeff at 321-5594 or Richard at 784-0528 and order one or more packs of this season's holiday cards. The price is $10.00 per packet of sixteen cards. Each pack contains four unique designs by local artists, with four units of each design. Each beautiful illustration is printed in rich black over royal blue in a snowy white background. The card interiors are blank,allowing you to create your own personal message. The back page makes the following quiet statement: "'Angels Among Us', an AIDS awareness project, an I.S.Q.C.C.B.E. fundraiser". Names of the artists, Joe Carr, Mary Mischenko, Dan Smith, and Glenn "Rocky" Woods, are also inscribed.

Yes, there are less expensive cards. But these cards make a statement about what your priorities are, and what kind of world you want this holiday season to find. Most importantly, all profits derived from these cards will be donated to A.V.O.C. Order now!

Merry Christmas

Happy Hanukkah

and Best Wishes for a

Joyous Holiday Season

filled with warm thoughts.

May health and happiness be

yours in the coming New Year!!!

World AIDS Day '96

Increasing Awareness Worldwide

December 1st the city of Cincinnati joined the world in observance of World AIDS Day, a day of events aimed at increasing AIDS awareness, honoring the memory of the *nearly one and a half million* persons who have died *this year alone*. We symbolically joined hands with others worldwide, to demonstrate to our governments and world leaders; to our pharmaceutical companies and medical authorities, that accelerated research continues to be necessary if a cure is ever to be found, and this increasingly indiscriminate killer is to be eradicated.

In San Francisco ceremonies were held unveiling the first national monument erected to honor the memory of the millions of individuals who have succumbed to AIDS. In Paris, France, more than 3,000 people took to the streets to call attention to this deadly disease and the need for increased government support of research.

Here in Cincinnati, our own Emperor, Ray Besse appeared on WXIX, Channel 19, discussing the day-to-day struggle of living with AIDS, and the need for increased awareness—especially among young adults who may still believe that this is a "gay" disease.

Current research indicates that HIV infection is growing much more quickly in the heterosexual population, with rates of infection among blacks and women increasing almost exponentially.

If it appears that World AIDS Day '96 was successful in achieving its goal, it is perhaps a paradox that this event will not completely be successful until the day that this event is used solely to honor the memories of those we have loved and lost. Only when we can live without fear for ourselves and our loved ones will this event be a complete success

People infected worldwide	22,000,000
People infected within the US	476,000
People infected in Hamilton County	964
AIDS Deaths to Date Hamilton County	614

In the summer of 1979, Marian Weage's son told her that he was gay. This led her to attend a Michigan PFLAG meeting to find information and support to combat the widespread negativity associated with being gay. She returned to her Cincinnati hometown in 1984 and convened the first meeting of PFLAG Cincinnati in August 1985 in the back room of Crazy Ladies Bookstore. In those early days, the group offered "Homemade Cookies and a Hug" to increase visibility and donations. During the AIDS crisis, this program became "Condoms and a Hug," with PFLAG members hitting the gay bars with piles of condoms and an attached note that read, "Wear this in good health. From your Moms and Dads at PFLAG." Today, PFLAG Cincinnati continues to provide vital support for lesbian, gay, bisexual, transgender, and intersex individuals, families, and friends in the same safe and caring environment created those many years ago. (Left, Scott Knox; below, Michael Chanak Jr.)

The Queen City Careers Association (QCCA) was founded in 1987 with the express purpose of promoting business and professionalism within and for the gay and lesbian community of Greater Cincinnati, providing a forum for gay and lesbian businesses and professionals to meet, and presenting educational opportunities on topics of interest to those professionals. Annual event highlights included multiple job/career fairs, trade shows, holiday gatherings, and even canoe outings for members. QCCA later became the Greater Cincinnati Gay Chamber of Commerce with the updated goals of strengthening relationships, creating networking opportunities, promoting Greater Cincinnati, and increasing the visibility of the area's LGBTQ community. (Both, Ron Clemons.)

Founded in New York City in 1987, ACT UP is a diverse, nonpartisan group of individuals united in anger and committed to ending the AIDS crisis. "Silence=Death," their famous slogan, epitomizes the need for direct action to make an actual difference. The Cincinnati chapter of ACT UP asserted its voice multiple times, staging various public events to demand attention to the disease that was ravaging our community. These demonstrations included their taking to the streets with placards ("April 30, 1989, 94200 and counting. 54,402 are dead") alongside the roaming figure of death, and their co-organizing of the 1991 protest against Sheriff Leis (described on page 65). (Both, Jeff Bixby.)

Cincinnati has been the home of myriad organizations working at the intersection of LGBTQ identity and education. In the late 1980s, Gays and Lesbians United for Education (GLUE) was formed. Originally created as a once-a-month social and support meeting for gay and lesbian teachers, the group quickly evolved into a more action-oriented organization: sending out informational newsletters and planning educational workshops. In 1994, the Gay and Lesbian Independent School Teacher Network (GLISTN) became a national organization and eventually supplanted GLUE. Then in 1997, GLISTN became GLSEN: Gay, Lesbian, and Straight Education Network, in order to pull in ally teachers. No matter the name, the goal has always been the same: creating the most supportive and safest possible school climate for all students and teachers. (Above, Jeff Bixby; below, Michael Chanak Jr.)

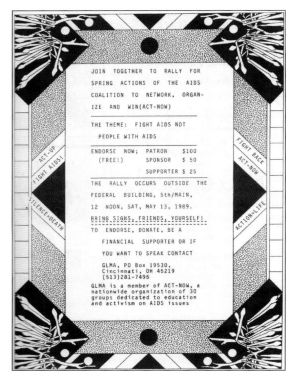

Following the 1987 March on Washington, many LGBTQ organizations were created in cities across the country. One of them was Gay and Lesbian March Activists (GLMA), a Cincinnati group wholly focused on marshaling energy toward action. A member of ACT-NOW, a nationwide organization of 30 different groups, GLMA organized various rallies and events dedicated to education and activism on AIDS-related issues. (Ohio Lesbian Archives.)

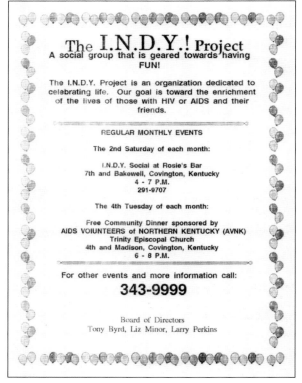

In the early 1990s, glimpses began to emerge that AIDS might not be the iron-clad death sentence that the avalanche of obituaries the 1980s promised it would be. One group popped up that was simply unthinkable a few years earlier: the I'm Not Dead Yet (INDY) Project was dedicated to the idea of celebrating life through creating social opportunities to share food, fellowship, and fun. (Jeff Bixby.)

Built from the simple (yet powerful) concept of providing the opportunity for gay and gay-supportive men to sing together and create positive change through music, the Cincinnati Gay Men's Chorus has been dazzling concertgoers for decades. They first rehearsed on October 1, 1991, bringing together 60 men from all walks of life: friends and strangers, young and old, gay and gay supportive. With every note, they embody their mission of striving for excellence, supporting and nurturing their members, entertaining their audiences, and working for justice, inclusion, and harmony between the LGBTQ community and the community at large. Whether performing at Pride festivals, the Walk to Stop AIDS, or their thrice annual conference, the chorus will continue to enrich lives through song as long as they have more notes to sing. (Both, Cincinnati Men's Chorus.)

What would a parade be without the 76 trombones? Okay, well, maybe the Queen City Rainbow Band (QCRB) has never featured quite so many, but the LGBTQ and ally band still provided countless tunes that have most certainly led the big parade. Founded in 2002 with a vision of promoting unity, generating pride, and providing education through music and visual performance, QCRB was a regular feature both at Cincinnati Pride as well as various other community events in the Greater Cincinnati area. A member of the Lesbian and Gay Band Association, QCRB members ranged in age and musical ability, and they proudly trumpeted their commitment to inclusion so that individuals would want to join, participate, and stay in the band. QCRB played its last note in 2015 before being disbanded. (Both, Ron Clemons.)

When JAC Stringer was a student at the University of Cincinnati (UC) in 2006, he saw a lack of representation and was inspired to form GenderBloc, a student group centered on trans activism. GenderBloc inspired some core changes at UC, including increased protections for gender identity/expression and an annual drag show, the first-ever hosted at any of the city's colleges and universities. When Stringer graduated, he started a project in 2008 that became Midwest Trans and Queer Wellness Initiative (MTQWI), which was eventually renamed Heartland Trans Wellness Group. These organizations hosted numerous social and educational opportunities, including Cincinnati Trans Community Group, TEENSPACE (for trans youth and their families), a trans night, a partner night, and a community night, all in the effort of centering and lifting up the trans voice within the Cincinnati LGBTQ narrative. (Both, JAC Stringer.)

Despite the ubiquitous narrative that being gay and holding a strong faith-based identity are mutually exclusive, the assertion could not be farther from the truth, even in as faith-centered and seemingly conservative a community as Cincinnati. Various houses of worship and faith organizations have been there every step of the way supporting the Cincinnati LGBTQ community: marching in Pride, standing side-by-side at protests with pro-equality placards aloft, and always attending to the spiritual health and well-being of everyone in Cincinnati so desperately fighting for equality. Notable supporters have included (but are certainly not limited to) New Spirit Oasis Metropolitan Community Church, Clifton United Methodist, Mt. Auburn Presbyterian, St. John's Unitarian, Trinity Episcopal, Church of our Saviour, Christ Church Cathedral, and St. John United Church of Christ. (Left, Caracole; below, Ohio Lesbian Archives.)

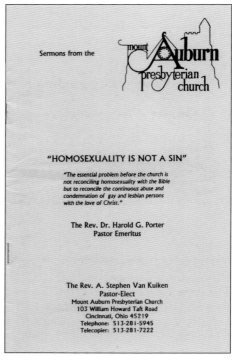

Sermons from the **mount Auburn presbyterian church**

"HOMOSEXUALITY IS NOT A SIN"

"The essential problem before the church is not reconciling homosexuality with the Bible but to reconcile the continuous abuse and condemnation of gay and lesbian persons with the love of Christ."

The Rev. Dr. Harold G. Porter
Pastor Emeritus

The Rev. A. Stephen Van Kuiken
Pastor-Elect
Mount Auburn Presbyterian Church
103 William Howard Taft Road
Cincinnati, Ohio 45219
Telephone: 513-281-5945
Telecopier: 513-281-7222

Before the black-tie galas were de rigueur, the Greater Cincinnati Chapter of Human Rights Campaign (HRC) was a distinctly more grassroots affair. Founded by Steve Endean in 1980 as one of the first gay and lesbian political action committees in the United States, HRC is now one of the largest civil rights organizations in the world. The Cincinnati chapter strives to end discrimination against LGBTQ people locally and realize a world that achieves fundamental fairness and equality for all. (Ron Clemons.)

The Abbey of the Immaculate 4-Way became a fully professed house of the legendary Sisters of Perpetual Indulgence in 2018, working diligently to be a source of joy and love in the Cincinnati LGBTQ community and the community at large. Originally formed in San Francisco in the late 1970s, the original Sisters quickly became known for their creative activism and ability to raise much-needed funds in truly dire times. (Ty Wesselkamper.)

For a corporate entity to make it onto these pages, they need to have really gone above and beyond. And Procter & Gamble has done just that. Their journey to support LGBTQ equality began in 1987 when employee Michael Chanak Jr. approached the chief equal employment opportunity officer to ask for LGBTQ employment protections. In 1992, the company announced that its anti-discrimination policies would include sexual orientation, becoming one of the first Fortune 500 companies to do so. Since that time, P&G has been at the vanguard of LGBTQ advocacy. Gay, Ally, Bisexual and Lesbian Employees of P&G (GABLE) was formed in 1996 and continues to help shape a culture where everyone can be their authentic selves. P&G was also a hugely vocal proponent of repealing Article XII, putting their money where their mouths were by ponying up large sums of funds to help achieve fairness for their LGBTQ employees and Cincinnati at large. (Above, Michael Chanak Jr.; below, Lisa Schreihart.)

Two

WE GATHER

SPACES AND EVENTS

The Cincinnati LGBTQ community has physically come together in a broad range of ways. Whether putting on their Sunday's best to attend the annual Stonewall Dinner, donning distinctly more casual clothing to congregate in the Golden Lion's Lounge, or getting ready to bowl the perfect score at CINTIT, these events and spaces provide a vivid illustration of the sheer power of strength in numbers. (Ron Clemons.)

It is impossible to overestimate the importance of Crazy Ladies Bookstore as a much-needed refuge, a widely-visited gathering place, an invaluable resource, and a vital hub for the Cincinnati LGBTQ community. Originally formed in 1978 as a private venture bravely serving the feminist community, the store became a collective in 1982 to keep the space in operation when the owner moved out of town. Named in honor of historical women who were deemed troublemakers and "crazy ladies" as a way to dismiss their power, Crazy Ladies Bookstore was so much more than an incredible retail space that centered the experience of women. For almost 25 years, this Cincinnati gem was a place where one could regularly tap into the spirit of community activism, be inspired by a visiting author using their words to make a difference, learn more about how individuals can create lasting change, or simply lounge around in a sea of like-minded people who wanted to make the world a better place. (Both, Ohio Lesbian Archives.)

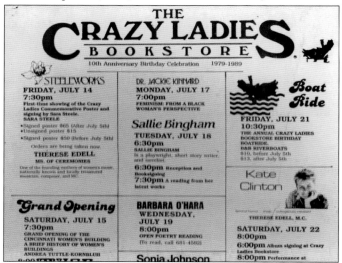

The Cincinnati Women's Building may have appeared to be a structure of bricks and mortar, but coursing through the structure was a more intangible ethos that truly changed lives. Physically, the building housed Crazy Ladies Bookstore, Ohio Lesbian Archives, Stonewall Human Rights Organization of Greater Cincinnati, and some programming space. But more than that, the energy in the building provided a nonsexist environment that fostered productivity, creativity, spirituality, and health; promoted feminist consciousness in all of its diversity; and opposed sexism, racism, homophobia, and other forms of discrimination. As a center for the lesbian community and all feminists, the Cincinnati Women's Building offered a safe space where diverse groups of women and their allies came together for discussion, work, and education. (Both, Ohio Lesbian Archives.)

"Badlands' dance floor is known as one of the best in the area. The men dance on, obvious in the stop-go staccato of the strobe. They bump and shake and shimmy, their attention riveted on the motion and each other. Out there are scores of continuing stories of romances lost and broken, passions kindled, even love. It's a hydra-headed soap opera with an all-male cast. It's not nearly as flashy or ostentatious up the hill in Clifton at Adam's Rib. It's your basic beer, pinball and pool table place. Women dance with one another upstairs, and sit around talking and drinking downstairs. The motif is very casual, jeans and workshirts mostly. Not very plush or exotic. But it's the only lesbian bar in town, so if you're a lesbian, it will have to do." *Cincinnati Enquirer*, Apil 4, 1982. (Left, David Wolff; below, Ohio Lesbian Archives.)

The April 4, 1982, *Cincinnati Enquirer* article continues, "And it's all happening right here in this river city. Every Saturday night homosexuals dress up and go dancing, drinking—celebrating the gay life. After an entire week living in a world where homosexuality is freakish at best, where feelings must be kept under wraps and every gesture may be suspect, on Saturday night, homosexuals only have to walk through the magic doorway and everything is turned upside down. All the assumptions are gay assumptions. All the conversations start where the outside conversations never even go. For the brief time spent inside the gay bar, gay men and women can cast side the burden of their unacceptability. Right or wrong, they can be gay without pretense . . . a universe all their own." (Both, David Wolff.)

ALLEY CAT

Cincinnati's only gay owned and operated disco, lounge & restaurant run exclusively for the gay communi

behind the Palace Theatre
616 Lodge

"PRIDE DAY CELEBRATION"

June 28, Sunday,
"Double Your Pleasure"
Buffet by donation for
Gay Community Switchboard

THANKS FOR MAKING OUR 2ND
ANNIVERSARY PARTY SUCH A SUCCESS!

WATCH FOR OUR COUNTRY &
WESTERN WEEKEND IN JUNE

DOUBLE YOUR PLEASURE
Wed. 10-Midnight & Sun. 4-7 pm

DISCO EVERY WED.-SUN. 9:30 - 2:30 am
SPECIALS TO THE LEVI & LEATHER'S
ON THURSDAY IN THE DISCO

Stop in for information
on other special events to come

421-

The Cincinnati Tri-State International tournament (CINTIT) has been providing so much more than bowling since its inception in the early 1980s. After organizers approached several different venues, only Mergard's, an African American–owned bowling alley, agreed to host the event. After the tournament, a banquet was held in the basement, complete with a trophy presentation, dinner, and dancing, all capping off one of the most well-attended LGBTQ events each and every year. Originally, organizers needed to convince local hotels to offer space and special rates, warning them that they would see guests in various modes of dress, but promising them solid sales at the hotel bar (which sealed the deal). Now four decades later, the event still draws competitors from all over the region for a tournament filled with fellowship, fundraising for various local nonprofits, and some of the best team shirts (and clever team names) ever seen in a bowling alley. (Both, Ron Clemons.)

Created in 1989 and situated in a third-floor room above Crazy Ladies Bookstore, the Ohio Lesbian Archives (OLA) stands as one of the only lesbian archives in the United States and the only known collection of its kind in the Ohio-Kentucky-Indiana region. For over 30 years, OLA has been collecting books, periodicals, music, photographs, posters, and regalia focused on lesbian history. Their collection includes LGBTQ histories and myriad other materials. More than a reference library, OLA has evolved into a veritable museum with trophies, political buttons, statues, gay history card games, and so much more. After Crazy Ladies closed in 2002, OLA moved to the Clifton United Methodist Church in 2006, where it welcomes students, researchers, and anyone looking to learn more about our vibrant history. (Both, Ohio Lesbian Archives.)

The AIDS Walk in Cincinnati stands today as one of the longest-running AIDS Walks still in existence both in Ohio and in the entire country. The event has gone through a series of names over the years (Red Ribbon Walk for AIDS, Cincy Walk to STOP AIDS, Caracole's Run/Walk for AIDS, and more), and has been sponsored at different times by AVOC, STOP AIDS, and Caracole. But no matter the name and no matter the sponsoring organization, the goal has remained the same: to raise much-needed funds and make a public statement about the importance of fighting AIDS. So many of these events have disappeared all over the nation due to lower participation and a declining sense of urgency. But the AIDS Walk in Cincinnati has persisted, raising millions of dollars and walking countless steps past the complacency, past the stigma, past the resistance, and straight on to a future where AIDS is no more. (Both, Ron Clemons.)

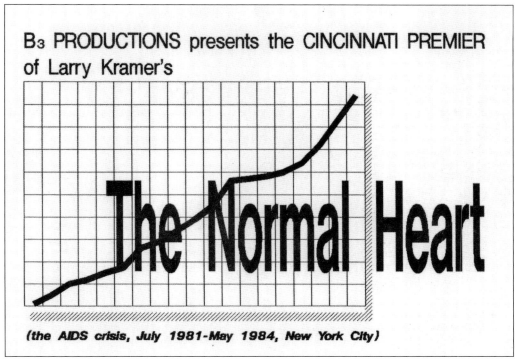

B₃ PRODUCTIONS presents the CINCINNATI PREMIER of Larry Kramer's

The Normal Heart

(the AIDS crisis, July 1981-May 1984, New York City)

Not quite four years after its first publication, the Cincinnati premiere of Larry Kramer's *The Normal Heart* was held in 1989. Depicting the rise of AIDS in New York City between July 1981 and May 1984, the program for the Cincinnati production featured the "1988 Annual Report of the STD/AIDS Control and Prevention Programs" of the Clement Health Center, which revealed a near tripling of new AIDS cases in Cincinnati from 1986 to 1987, and an increase of AIDS-related deaths from year to year. Jeff Bixby, one of the show's producers, wrote to the Cincinnati Commissioner of Health asking for an endorsement of the production. The reply highlighted that "some portions of the play depicting the gay lifestyle may be received as controversial in the Cincinnati community" but that it would overall be an important contribution to the public discourse on the health crisis. Nevertheless, Commissioner Broadnax concluded that "it would not be appropriate for the Health Department to endorse this play." (Both, Jeff Bixby.)

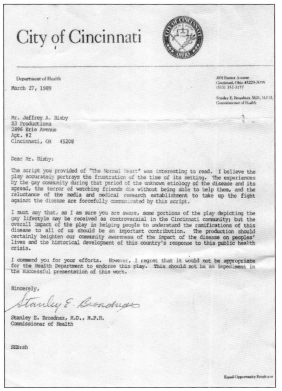

Scholar and civil rights advocate Kimberlé Williams Crenshaw once said, "The way we imagine discrimination or disempowerment is more complicated for people who are subjected to multiple forms of exclusion. The good news is that intersectionality provides us a way to see it." Countless events in Cincinnati have provided the opportunity to explore the theme of intersectionality: discussions, screenings, roundtables, and more made space for individuals to express their whole identity as opposed to solely one aspect of their being. Whether it was an open meeting to simultaneously eradicate homophobia and racism or an evening with an author who writes at the crossroads of faith, sexuality, and feminism, these events painted a far more complete picture of authenticity than the narrow lens of solely looking at sexual orientation alone. (Both, Ohio Lesbian Archives.)

Thursday, February 13 1985
Adar 4 5746

HILLEL HOUSE
&
NEW JEWISH AGENDA
present

Hillel House
2615 Clifton Ave.
8:00 P.M.

AN EVENING WITH
POET & NOVELIST

MARGE PIERCY

Marge Piercy, a poet and novelist widely acclaimed for the exploration of women's and Jewish themes in her work, is the Elliston Poetry Foundation's resident writer for the winter quarter. Her most recent poetry collection is My Mother's Body, published in 1985 by Knopf. Circles in the Water, an edition of selected poems, was released in 1982. Other poetry collections include Breaking Camp, Hard Loving, Living in the Open, and The Moon is Always Female. Her novels include Braided Lives, Fly Away Home, Vida, and Woman on the Edge of Time. She has, in addition, published a non-fiction book entitled Parti-Colored Blocks for a Quilt.

In her Hillel reading, Ms. Piercy will be reading from her poetry and from her novel-in-progress, part of which has been published in Lilith.

hillel house 221-6728
new jewish agenda 421-6650
or 751-0926

labor donated

One of the largest LGBTQ events of the year for decades, the Stonewall Dinner was an evening that the entire community looked forward to all year long. The dinner provided a unique opportunity for the LGBTQ community to come together and rub elbows with supportive politicians and civic leaders, to honor human rights, and to celebrate the LGBTQ community's achievements through impassioned speeches and words of recognition. Attendees enjoyed fine food and a substantive, lively, and entertaining program. After years of extraordinarily successful events, the 2001 dinner proved to be disastrous: event attendance was low due to moving the date to an already packed Pride month, and Stonewall Cincinnati took in $4,600 of the projected $30,000. That said, not one of the 600 attendees asked for a refund when entertainer Sandra Bernhard had to cancel at the last minute. (Both, Ron Clemons.)

STONEWALL CINCINNATI
PRESENTS
AN EVENING WITH

Helen Gallagher

PRESIDENT M.O.H.R.
(MICHIGAN ORGANIZATION FOR HUMAN RIGHTS)

4TH ANNUAL
DINNER/DANCE
QUALITY INN • RIVERVIEW • COVINGTON, KENTUCKY

SATURDAY, APRIL 19, 1986

The 18th Annual
Stonewall Dinner Party
Saturday, April 8th, 2000

We hope you enjoy this
Mega-makeover of an evening,
here at Cincinnati's
Music Hall Ballroom.

Stonewall Cincinnati
P.O. Box 954 · Cincinnati, OH 45201
513.651.2500
www.stonewallcincinnati.org

For years, Caracole operated the Caracole Recovery Community in Cincinnati's Roselawn neighborhood, a congregate living community for chemically dependent individuals living with HIV/AIDS who were in an intentional recovery program. This critically important program allowed people to seek their own healthy path forward in a judgment-free space surrounded by others engaged in the same journey. (Ron Clemons.)

On September 17, 1993, the bylaws were signed on the Gay and Lesbian Community Center of Greater Cincinnati, the next evolution of GCGLC. The center opened in December 1993 at Longworth Hall off of Pete Rose Way, then moved to 230 East Ninth Street in 1996, and finally to 4119 Hamilton Avenue in Northside from 1998 until the doors closed in 2013. The space was a center of programming, a center of Pride preparations, and most certainly, a center of community activity and coordination. (Michael Chanak Jr.)

The first Mr. Tri-State contest was held in 2000 and was originally the idea of Nigel Cotterill (Mr. Miami Valley Leather 1997, Mr. Queen City Leather 2003) and his boy at the time, Andrew Keisker (Ohio Drummerboy 2000, Great Lakes Drummerboy 2000). The event was designed to bring together the leather groups and organizations of Southwest Ohio, Kentucky, and Indiana to celebrate the leather lifestyle and foster support and visibility for the entire regional leather community. The winner of the Mr. Tri-State contest went on to compete at International Mr. Leather. The first Mr. Tri-State, Mike Taylor, actually went on to win the title of International Mr. Leather 2001. The original title sash was officially donated to the Leather Archives and Museum in 2004. After the 2004 contest, the weekend went on hiatus until it was brought back in 2010 by Scorpius of Cincinnati and then by Ron Clemons in 2011. (Both, Ron Clemons.)

The December 1 observance of World AIDS Day has long been recognized in Cincinnati, including at the 2000 commemoration pictured here held at the Community Center in Newport, Kentucky, which featured choral performances, art creation, candle-lighting, and impassioned words from local leaders about where we have been with the ravages of AIDS and where we still need to go for a future without the disease. Founded in 1988, World AIDS Day was the first-ever global health day and provides an opportunity for people worldwide to unite in the fight against HIV and to lift up the voices of those who are living with HIV/AIDS as well as those who have died from an AIDS-related illness. The day unites those in Cincinnati with those around the world trying to raise money, increase awareness, fight prejudice, and improve education. (Both, Ron Clemons.)

In the spirit of the Harlem Renaissance, the Eyes Open Festival was created to celebrate and foster an understanding of the arts in the black lesbian and gay community. First held in 2008, the event coincided with the opening of the NAACP National Convention in Cincinnati and featured visual and performance art by black LGBTQ artists. The goals of the Eyes Open Festival were to grant an outlet for black LGBTQ artists; to bring awareness to a vibrant, yet relatively invisible, cultural movement to the public; to create dialogue between the black LGBTQ community and other communities; to explore and celebrate diversity; and to foster understanding. The Eyes Open Festival was held the subsequent year in 2009 and featured paintings, sculptures, a film festival, musical performers, and an overall opportunity for Cincinnati to celebrate black LGBTQ artists. (Both, Doug Cooper Smith.)

Seeing LGBTQ lives up on the big screen creates an opportunity like no other to see our stories presented in unique and compelling ways. Screening a whole batch of films with LGBTQ content ups that ante tremendously. Created in 2012, OutReels Cincinnati fosters a creative outlet for the tri-state area where LGBTQ issues are expressed and discussed through the art of film. With hundreds of films screened at their festival, the event has been held at the Know Theatre, the Aronoff Center for the Arts, the Warsaw Federal Incline Theater, and most recently, at the Garfield Theatre. Submissions come in from all around the world, and many of the screenings have featured talkbacks with notable producers, directors, and actors. (Both, David Wolff.)

On June 7, 2017, Jim Obergefell tore the paper off a new street sign reading "John Arthur and Jim Obergefell Way" at the corner of Mercer Street and Vine Street. The street sign honors the couple who lived on the street before Arthur died in 2013, and Obergefell filed a lawsuit challenging Ohio's ban on same-sex marriage after the state refused to put his name on his husband's death certificate. Their case was combined with lawsuits filed by 32 couples, children, and widowers in four states. As Obergefell's lawsuit had the lowest case number, his name was listed first, forever enshrining the case as *Obergefell v. Hodges* (Richard Hodges was the Director of the Ohio Department of Health that oversaw death certificates). The Supreme Court ruled on June 26, 2015, that the Equal Protection Clause and the Due Process Clause of the 14th Amendment to the US Constitution granted same-sex couples the fundamental right to marry. (David Wolff.)

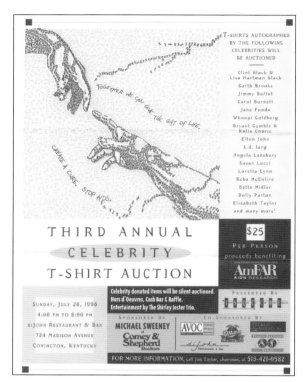

An annual highlight in Cincinnati was the celebrity t-shirt auction presented by the Imperial Sovereign Queen City Court of the Buckeye Empire Inc. and benefitting such organizations as AVOC and amFAR. In addition to the dinner and musical performances (including being serenaded one year by Broadway legend Jennifer Holliday), there was a live auction featuring one-of-a-kind t-shirts signed by such celebrities as Madonna, Cher, Elizabeth Taylor, Dolly Parton, and Tom Hanks. (Jeff Bixby.)

On August 30, 2018, a red, orange, yellow, green, blue, indigo, and violet crosswalk was installed at Twelfth and Vine Streets in Over-the-Rhine. The idea was proposed by Councilman Chris Seelbach in 2017. An anonymous donor covered the $8,000 cost of the crosswalk, and it was designed by the Cincinnati Department of Transportation. More than 100 cities across the United States now feature Pride crosswalks. (David Wolff.)

Three

WE COMMUNICATE
MEDIA

Community and connection don't always happen in person. They can also be effectively created via sources of media. Through newspapers, radio, newsletters, and television, the LGBTQ community has wielded every method at their disposal to reach every individual in every corner of Cincinnati. Increasingly, stories appeared in the mainstream press, highlighting both victories and struggles. (Ohio Lesbian Archives.)

$1.50   **dinah**   JANUARY/FEBRUARY 1990

P.O. BOX 1485
CINCINNATI, OHIO 45201

"Good Friends" On Channel 10

A lesbian talk show is now appearing on Channel 10 of community access T.V. "Good Friends" features Therese Edell as host. One show has aired so far and another has been taped. The show spotlights women in the women's community, with interviews and performances. The first show featured Estelle Riley of Kate & Company, and performer Mary Kroner, who played two of her compositions on guitar. Therese has MC'd at local coffeehouses and for music festivals around the country. She is known as "The Voice" of the Michigan Womyn's Music Festival and is a natural interviewer and talk show host.

I had the honor of attending the taping for the second show at Warner Cable.

Lisa Kaiser, local attorney, discussed the 1990 Gay Games, which will be held in Vancouver, British Columbia this year. She is the media contact for the local Gay Games Committee. Besides sports, the Games will feature cultural attractions including a 1000 voice chorus, a band, a "Chefs of the World" event, square dancing and chamber music. Lisa stressed that all are welcome to participate, regardless of athletic ability. Said Kaiser, "Inclusion is the name of the game." See Lisa's article in this issue of DINAH for more information and for area contacts. During the second half of the program, dancer Gloria Esenwein talked about her dance background, her work as a teacher and choreographer, and performed a dance while singing a Karla Bonoff song, "Home".

The first show, with Estelle Riley and Mary Kroner, appears throughout January on Channel 10 Tuesdays at 11pm, Wednesdays at 9pm, and Fridays at 11pm. The second show, with Lisa Kaiser and Gloria Esenwein, will air Tuesdays and Fridays at 11pm throughout February. More shows are planned. It's about time we got something like this on TV!

(Continued on p. 5)

INSIDE:

National Lesbian Conference   p. 3
Gay Games/Cultural Festival   p. 4
Phranc at Canal Street   p. 6
Community Interview   p. 7
Advice   p. 8

AND MORE!!!!!

"GOOD FRIENDS"

1

First hitting the airwaves in 1974, *Alternating Currents* originally broadcast from WAIF, a locally run, non-syndicated community radio station in Walnut Hills. The LGBTQ public affairs program covered everything from local and national news; interviews with LGBTQ figures on the national, regional, and local stage; the latest event announcements; and music that set your feet to tapping. Because it was the only way to access LGBTQ content on the radio waves, local residents remember inventing errands so they could be in their cars to hear the programming. In 2010, *Alternating Currents* moved to WVQC, a lower power (LP) station in downtown Cincinnati. Unfortunately, it was so LP that the signal could not get past the hills of Kentucky or out to the suburbs. *Alternating Currents* finally went off the air in 2012 and holds the incredible distinction of being the second-longest-running LGBTQ radio show in the United States. (Both, Cheryl Eagleson.)

Originally published under the name *Dinosaur News* by the Lesbian Activist Bureau, *Dinah* was reborn under its new name in 1975. The grassroots newsletter with an all-volunteer staff featured articles, short stories, poetry, and letters covering womanhood, lesbianism, race, family, sex, music, literature, and everything in between. *Dinah* sponsored events, meetings, potlucks, protests against discrimination and domestic violence, and even a winning season in the city league softball championship. Captured in ink are the voices and stories of lesbians who were not given their proper due in other gay media, even as Dinah provided a platform to bring the community closer together both on and off the page. The newsletter lasted an incredible 22 years and 100 issues, finally ceasing publication in 1997. (Both, Ohio Lesbian Archives.)

"DEPROGRAM" LESBIANS?

dinah special report
on homophobia

May 1, 1982

ATTENTION: Lesbian, Gay, and Feminist Bookstores, Periodicals, and Organizations

From: The Cincinnati Lesbian Activist Bureau, P.O. Box 1485, Cincinnati, OH 45201

In Hamilton County Common Pleas Court April 12–April 23 Ted Patrick, Naomi Goss, and James Roe were tried in connection with the October 1981 abduction of 19-year-old Stephanie Riethmiller. Her mother was also indicted but was not tried. Instead both parents were given immunity in exchange for their testimony. Midway through the trial Judge Gilbert Bettman granted defense motions to drop sexual battery charges against Goss and Patrick and kidnapping charges against all three. At the end of a two week trial the jury found all three defendants innocent of assault, Mr. Roe innocent of sexual battery, and Patrick innocent of abduction. Both Goss and Roe will be tried again on the abduction charge as the jury was hopelessly deadlocked. The prosecuting attorney, Simon Leis, is well-known for his affiliation with the Moral Majority and his loathing of homosexuals. Lesbian and Gay observers at the trial commented on Leis' defense of the parents and his attempts to discover whether or not Stephanie Riethmiller and Patricia Thiemann are in fact lesbians. Both gay and straight observers were heard wondering who was in fact on trial—the defendants or the two victims?

What follows is a brief summary of the case, quotes from the trial, and quotes from Cincinnati reporters and others both during and after the trial. It will become obvious why members of the Cincinnati Lesbian Activist Bureau, the local gay men, and other concerned and freedom-loving citizens are outraged by the trial and the gross injustices and the terrible implications if the results of this case go unchallenged. It was obvious to gay and lesbian observers at the trial that homophobia was used by the defense and the prosecution to obscure and block the path of justice. The victims were treated as criminals (the crime? suspected lesbianism) and the principals were granted immunity from prosecution and their hirelings acquitted.

On October 8, 1981 Stephanie Riethmiller and her roommate, Patricia Thiemann, arrived home from work at the usual time: 5:15 p.m. Two men approached, asking for directions, then sprayed Patricia with mace and pushed her while the other man pulled Stephanie into a waiting van. Stephanie's father was waiting inside, Naomi Goss drove, and the other two men, James Roe and Ray (still at large) jumped in beside Stephanie and her father.

The Riethmiller case not only shocked the LGBTQ community in Cincinnati but also stoked fears far outside the region as the unbelievable story was quickly amplified to a global audience. In October 1981, nineteen-year-old Stephanie Riethmiller was abducted outside of her Norwood home, wrestled into a van, and taken to a house in Alabama for "deprogramming." Investigators quickly learned that her parents had paid $8,000 to "free" their daughter from her roommate's alleged "mind control" and "lesbian relationship." The ensuing two-week trial of Riethmiller's parents was a mess. The prosecuting attorney, a well-known associate of the antigay Moral Majority, spent more time questioning whether Stephanie was a lesbian (bolstering her parents' homophobic defense) than he did presenting a case against her parents, who were both found not guilty of the assault charges. The case was covered by both local media as well as national outlets like the *New York Times*, leaving LGBTQ observers around the country wondering who really was on trial in this tragic case. (Both, Ohio Lesbian Archives.)

Riethmiller Case Reflections

(Cincinnati Enquirer 5/7/82)

BY RICHARD RASKIN
Guest Columnist — used by permission

The author is a free-lance writer and editor who has written articles on the Riethmiller case for the Progressive and New Age magazines. In addition he has been a frequent contributor of book reviews in The Enquirer. This fall he plans to enter the University of Cincinnati College of Law as a first-year student.

DESPITE HIS FAILURE to win a single conviction, Hamilton County Prosecutor Simon L. Leis Jr. has already reaped several rounds of praise for his performance in the recent trial of Stephanie Riethmiller's deprogrammers. It's no wonder that most of that praise comes from the defendants and their attorneys — Leis presented a case which it was nearly impossible for them to lose.

By now the basic events surrounding Stephanie Riethmiller's deprogramming should be familiar to readers. In October of last year she was grabbed outside her Norwood home and taken to a house in Alabama for deprogramming. During the ensuing week, investigators learned that Stephanie's parents, William and Martha Riethmiller of Indian Hill, had paid deprogrammers $8,000 to free their daughter of her roommate's alleged "mind control." It also became evident that Stephanie's parents feared she was a lesbian.

LET'S LOOK first at the parents' two motives for having Stephanie deprogrammed: lesbianism and mind control. At first glance there is no discernible relationship between the two issues. But for parents who believe that their child is homosexual, and that homosexuality is a sin, and that their child is not a sinner, the theory of mind control reconciles the apparent conflicts neatly. Ted Patrick, in fact, has used this reasoning for years, despite the protests of psychiatrists, to justify deprogramming.

To the Riethmillers, Stephanie's roommate was a demon and the deprogrammers were merely exorcists. Stephanie was merely a passive receptacle of evil, waiting to be emptied.

When it came time to prepare for trial, Leis and Assistant Prosecutor Arthur Ney took to the Riethmillers' mind-control theory and swallowed it whole. A list of particulars they filed in December presented an elaborate defense of the parents' moral vigilantism, portraying Stephanie as a lesbian controlled by the "dominant force" of her supposed lover (in accordance with the myth that all homosexual relationships take on dominant/passive roles), while

Riethmillers as "concerned parents" who contacted deprogrammers "out of a sense of frustration." No one who saw the document could have been surprised when the Riethmillers were granted immunity from prosecution.

WHY DID the prosecution consider Stephanie's sexual preference relevant to the case? Why did they take such pains to exonerate her parents? Leis was preparing to grind a homophobic ax in court.

And he did in his opening remarks on April 14. Reiterating the arguments made in the bill of particulars, Leis set the stage for a Kafkaesque spectacle of prosecution and defense uniting in common purpose to malign the victim. But Judge Gilbert Bettman pulled the rug out from under both sides with the announcement that testimony regarding Stephanie and her roommate's sexual lives would not be permitted.

The prosecution's pre-trial strategy had to be scrapped. An empty train had been derailed.

While the defense rebounded quickly, Leis and Ney were never able to get back on track after this initial setback. (But was it a setback? Would their case against the deprogrammers have been fortified by the revelation of Stephanie's sexual preference?) Having based their entire case on a fatuous issue, they were now faced with finding a focus to their argument. And a funny thing happened: Suddenly Ney and Leis were protecting the victim, arguing her case, objecting to improper defense questioning as the prosecution should. For a moment it seemed that justice might be served after all.

EVENTS PROVED otherwise. The defense was able to raise numerous questions about the prosecution's version of the story. Why did Stephanie, upon returning to Cincinnati, say she had had a "positive experience" in Alabama? If she had been raped, why did she not resist her attacker and why did she not mention it immediately upon returning?

To the victim's misfortune, the prosecution was ill-prepared to face such questions, even though answers were readily available. Many prisoners come to sympathize and agree with their abductors; witness Patty Hearst. She took on the values of her abductors only to revert to her original beliefs not long after her release. Apparently this is what happened to Stephanie Riethmiller. The trauma of her deprogramming was enough to temporarily jar her convictions. It should not be surprising at all that for 24 hours after returning, Stephanie "agreed" with her captors.

prosecution did not call on expert witnesses to testify to this phenomenon.

EXPERTS COULD also have testified to the fact that victims of rape frequently do not understand the nature of the crime committed against them for some time after the fact. It is perfectly plausible that Stephanie Riethmiller did not know herself that she had been raped until she spoke to the Norwood police. Yet the defense argued that the police planted this idea in her mind (thus accomplishing in a few hours what Ted Patrick's henchmen had failed to do in a week) and the prosecution was stumped. They pursued the charge of sexual battery with less vigor henceforth and it is no wonder they could not persuade a jury to convict.

Also, many rape victims do not scream and fight in resistance, particularly if they are trapped in a situation where resistance is useless. This does not mean that they "want it," as James Roe's attorney Thomas Miller suggested, nor does it mean they relinquish their right to legal protection. Unfortunately, it does mean they are liable to be further victimized in the courtroom. But, again, expert testimony and a more sophisticated argument could have mitigated this circumstance.

TO SOMEONE who sat in the courtroom and heard her testify, the idea of Stephanie Riethmiller bouncing from the "control" of her mother to that of her roommate, to James Roe, to the police, to her attorney — like a mindless object — seemed patently absurd. On the stand, Stephanie was a tough, articulate witness, guarding her ground with carefully measured responses to questioning, wasting no words. Regrettably, the measures to enhance her credibility as a witness, thus undermining their own case, the defense, meanwhile, used every known tactic to denounce her. One had to think there was another, fuller story that was not being heard in this courtroom.

There was an ironic, if unwitting, accuracy to the way the news media referred to the case as "the Riethmiller trial." Though no Riethmillers were accused, if often seemed as though Stephanie's sexual preference were the real subject of the trial. This could have been prevented had the prosecution not been working at cross purposes — defending the parents, condemning the victim, and finally prosecuting the defendants.

ONCE AGAIN Prosecutor Leis' crusading moralism insulated not only the rights of his constituents but the effectiveness of his own office. This was not justice and it certainly was not

Jaws dropped all over the region in 1982 when the *Cincinnati Enquirer* ran a special 27-page section entitled "Homosexuals: A Cincinnati Report." In the lengthy explanation on the front-end of the package, the editors noted that the report was "an attempt to provide a context to understand the lives of perhaps 140,000 Cincinnatians who are gay." The 18-stories included pieces like "Homosexuals say repression in Greater Cincinnati creates fear and elaborate secrecy in their lives," "Gale Rose, once Cincinnati's leading gay madam, has two portraits on her mantle— one as woman, the other as a man," and "Most politicians in Greater Cincinnati welcome the homosexuals' secret votes, but not their public endorsements." A special section of this length in 1982 about the LGBTQ community from the city's paper of record was truly a stupefying increase in visibility, despite the public backlash and flood of letters to the editor (of which there were many). (Both, Ohio Lesbian Archives.)

The Whys Of Homosexuality

BY TOM SHRODER
and GREGG LEVOY

Stephen remembers growing up all-boy. He played baseball, took fool-hardy dares, and once helped cut a hole in the side of the girls' bunk at summer camp so he and his buddies could peek in at night. He thought anything pink, classical or without scars and scratches on the knees reeked of incipient queerness.

He had an All-American family: a dominant father, a deferring mother and a brother who was a pain in the neck—everything he needed for card-carrying membership in the macho culture.

When Stephen grew up, no one was more surprised than he that he fell in love with men instead of women.

Everything he had ever been taught—from the birds and the bees to the high school prom—told him he was all wrong. But no matter what he *thought*, there was no denying what he felt.

And that was the heart of the problem. The debate over homosex-uality can rage all around him, and it does, but after all the contradicting theories have advanced and retreated, Stephen and thousands of others in this city are left with being what one psychiatrist refers to as "obligatory homosexuals"—men and women whose sexual drive can *only* be fulfill-ed by members of their own sex. It is

The WALL
STONEWALL CINCINNATI's Newsletter

Education Advocacy Outreach "Working to tear down prejudice brick by brick."

Volume 1, Issue 4 — Proudly serving the Greater Cincinnati area since 1982 — August 6 , 2001

STONEWALL CINCINNATI:
Up Close & Personal

On July 18, Stonewall Cincinnati's Board of Directors issued a statement to members and supporters announcing their decision to eliminate the position of Executive Director of Stonewall effective August 10, 2001. The decision was based solely on the on-going financial constraints of the organization.

Doreen Cudnik, the Executive Director since September 1999, has done an excellent job of increasing the visibility and credibility of Stonewall and will be sorely missed. The Board of Stonewall has already begun the process of re-trenching, re-building and re-vitalizing their financial base and will be looking to the community for support in maintaining this vital voice for the GLBT community.

The following Questions and Answers provide additional information.

What has happened to Stonewall?

Due to a severe financial shortfall, Stonewall's Board has reluctantly eliminated the Executive Director position because

there was not enough money to fund it. This will be effective August 10, 2001.

Why is it being eliminated and who will do the work?

There simply is no money to pay the Executive Director's salary. The office will be maintained by Operations Manager, Dan Mess, part time, in the near term. Stonewall's program and project work will need to be assumed by Board members and volunteers.

What will happen to Doreen?

Doreen hopes to stay in Cincinnati and is seeking employment here. She plans to stay active in the GLBT community and continue her support of Stonewall's efforts.

Why did Stonewall run out of money?

The projected budget was based on previous year's receipts. Unfortunately, throughout the year results of fund raising efforts fell far short of our projected goals. This was especially true with Stonewall's recent Celebration evening, which is the primary fundraising event.

Why were revenues down from the Celebration event?

First, the event is designed both to be a fundraiser and a celebratory event for the GLBT community. Consequently the cost is kept low to financially enable as many people as possible to attend. There has been no increase in the basic ticket price for over 10 years. Second, the event was held in Covington to call attention to the harmful Issue 3 / Article XII situation in Cincinnati. The Covington Convention Center is a fine facility, but its contract required using its catering services which were far more expensive than past years when we have been able to get most of the food donated. Third, it was decided to make the Stonewall event part of the Pride festivities rather than holding it in April, its usual time. In retrospect, this was a mistake as many people were just "tired" from Pride activities and "short of funds" because of all the other Pride activities. Attendance was down significantly. Stonewall felt decisions on all three points were philosophically correct, but together they led to a serious financial shortfall.

How will Stonewall raise money?

Stonewall will try to step up its grant writing and increase membership, hold events, and simply ask for financial contributions from the GLBT community to keep its projects going.

What about the Stonewall building?

This is a tough one. Stonewall bought the building with its potential for multiple office and meeting spaces with the hope that it would develop into a home for many GLBT organizations. However, without the involvement of other community groups, it is unlikely that sufficient grants could be obtained to develop the building to its potential. Especially now with its financial problems, Stonewall does not have the money on its own to develop the building.

What can the GLBT community do at this time?

This is very important. The work that Stonewall does is essential to the GLBT community in Cincinnati. Those projects and programs and involvement

See Stonewall Up Close, page 2

Annual Meeting August 21

Stonewall Cincinnati will hold its Annual Membership Meeting on Tuesday, August 21 at 7 PM at the Stonewall office (1118 Race Street).

It is vitally important that all those interested in the future of Stonewall be at this meeting. Input and energy from Stonewall members, as well as those in the

community who have not in the past supported the organization, is critical at this time in Stonewall's history.

Agenda items will include the election of new board members, a discussion of organizational changes, a discussion of Stonewall's involvement in community racial issues, and an update

on the collaborative work between Stonewall and Citizens to Restore Fairness. CRF is the group that has been formed to lead the Article XII repeal effort.

Everyone who believes in the mission of Stonewall, which is, in part, to "end discrimination and violence [against gay, lesbian, bisexual, and transgender people], and to promote cultural inclusion through education, advocacy, and outreach" is encouraged to attend.

Call the Stonewall office at 513-651-2500 for more information.

ATTEND THIS MEETING !

Stonewall Cincinnati P.O. Box 954 Cincinnati Ohio 45201 Tel: 513-651-2500 Fax: 513-651-3044 www.stonewallcincinnati.org

1

Since their creation in 1982, Stonewall Human Rights Organization of Greater Cincinnati has sponsored various different types of publications in their efforts to engage with the local LGBTQ community. The most common was their newsletter: a mailer that alternated between a quarterly and monthly offering. More than just information and events of the organization, the newsletter also covered relevant national news and reflections from LGBTQ Cincinnatians. In 2001, the newsletter was rebranded *The Wall* under the tagline of "Working to tear down prejudice brick by brick." Stonewall Cincinnati also was the chief organization behind the 1998-launched *Greater Cincinnati GLBT News*, which ran for few years before moving to an online format. (Both, Jeff Bixby.)

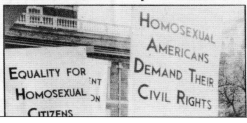

Issue 3, Yes or No — What to do? — page 2

INSIDE
Stonewall Cincinnati..........Page 2
Community Center.............Page 3
Financial Advisor..............Page 5
"I.N.D.Y!" Project..............Page 6
Its About Living..................Page 6
Organizations.....................Page 7

Greater Cincinnati October
GLBT News
Serving the Region's Gay, Lesbian, Bisexual and Transgender Residents
Voice Mail/FAX 513/665-6809   P.O. Box 14971, Cincinnati, OH 45250-0971   MAP Publications

Sunday, October 11 at the Mt. Lookout Cinema Grill
GLSEN hosts premiere of movie, "Out of the Past"

Busy with plans for the premiere of *Out of the Past*, we thought we would give you some background information on how this film came to be.

These are notes from the film's director, Jeff Dupre. Jeff was production coordinator on Ken Burn's film, The West, an eight-part documentary film series which aired on PBS in September 1996.

Out of the Past is his first film. We hope you get a chance to see this

determined that it should consist of five biographies spanning 300 years of American history, but we didn't know which ones to choose, nor did we know how we would string them together to create a coherent, dramatic arc.

I started to work on *Out of the Past* full-time in October of 1996. Michelle wrote a script and oversaw archival research and Eliza lent her considerable historical knowledge and ultimately became

Launching in the mid-1980s right when investment in the infrastructure and programming in networks was booming, Gay Cable Network (GCN) was the premiere cable television network catering to the LGBTQ community. GCN had bureaus in New York City, Dallas, Minneapolis, Miami, San Francisco, and yes, Cincinnati. The Cincinnati Bureau produced a wide range of segments that were incorporated into the GCN broadcast, from coverage of significant events to interviews with notable LGBTQ personalities, traveling all over the Midwest to capture stories that would interest their solid audience of viewers. Of particular note, the Cincinnati-produced segment "This Week in Gay History with Jeff Bixby" was a regular fixture on the national broadcasts, bringing forth the LGBTQ community's rich past to a present-day context. (Both, Jeff Bixby.)

THE YELLOW PAGE

P.O. Box 5009 Cincinnati, OH 45205 • (513) 851-3326

Serving Gays, Lesbians and Friends

λ

Vol. 6, Issue 7   PUBLISHED IN CINCINNATI, OHIO © 1984 The Yellow Page   **July, 1984**

λ

NATIONAL MARCH
FOR
LESBIAN/GAY RIGHTS
SAN FRANCISCO ▼ 1984

BRING GAY RIGHTS TO THE ATTENTION
OF THE DEMOCRATIC CONVENTION,
AND THE NATION.

National March For Lesbian & Gay Rights

history will be made in San Francisco not just for the Democratic Party but for the Lesbian/Gay Community as well. The National March for Lesbian and Gay Rights is planned to coincide with the Democratic National Convention. its purpose is to move Lesbian and Gay Issues to the center of the American political debate.

Monday, July 16th, the leadership of the Democratic Party will gather in San Francisco to select a candidate for President and to debate the issues which confront our nation. In attendance at this national convention will be approximately 20,000 media representatives reporting this debate to hundreds of millions of people. (Media audience to between 500 million and 1 billion, according to Roz Wyman, Executive Director of the Democratic National Convention.) The issue of the oppression of the Lesbian/Gay Community will be raised to millions of people. The pur-

The Yellow Page was published in Cincinnati for a few years in the late 1970s and early 1980s, and expanded service to Dayton in 1984. Under the tagline of "Serving Gays, Lesbians and Friends," the newspaper presented a wide swath of content: national LGBTQ news (usually on the front page), updates from various LGBTQ organizations in Cincinnati, photographs from events, and a "Health Comments by Dr. Bob" column, where readers could write in their questions, which were increasingly about HIV/AIDS. (Jeff Bixby.)

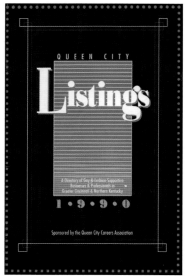

Published by the Queen City Careers Association and later by the Greater Cincinnati Gay Chamber of Commerce, *Listings* has served for decades as a directory to LGBTQ-supportive businesses, organizations, and resources in the area. As written in the 2019–2020 edition, "every time a business puts a rainbow flag in their window, or releases special Pride editions of their products, or places an ad in an LGBTQ publication, they are announcing to ALL of their customers that they believe in the rights and human dignity of the queer community." (Ohio Lesbian Archives.)

The Gay Beat launched on January 21, 1985, the same day as President Reagan's second inauguration. The two dates were not a coincidence. From their first issue: "This day marks another kind of inauguration as well, that of a local, gay news publication. . . . The purposes of The Gay Beat are these: to report the news; to educate the reading public about the issues which impact our community; and to help foster a collective, political agenda for the lesbian and gay male community of greater Cincinnati." Over its 10 years in print, The Gay Beat took many forms, from photocopied typed sheets to a newsletter appearance to more traditional newsprint. No matter what the form, the mission of informing LGBTQ Cincinnati residents helping to create a collective voice always remained the same. (Both, Ohio Lesbian Archives.)

The **Gay Beat**

covering issues of concern and events to the Queen City areas Lesbians and Gay Men

© 1985 GayBeat

Volume 1 Number 1   January 21, 1985

A STATEMENT OF PURPOSE

On January 21, 1985, we mark the second inauguration of Ronald Reagan as President of the United States. Here stands a man whose administration, party and constituency echo the most homophobic strain in American politics today. Yet he has carried the presidency with large numbers of individual gay people, from the very closeted to our very "leadership."

This day marks another kind of inauguration as well, that of a local, gay news publication, "The Gay Beat." Here, in the heart of the homophobic midwest, the beat goes on: the tradition of the free press, and of the free gay press in Cincinnati, Ohio, continues.

We pose two questions for our readers. What is happening to gay men and lesbians as we live out our private lives in this society, this community? And what do gay people want as gay people, as a community within this society?

The purposes of The Gay Beat are these: to report the news; to educate the reading public about the issues which impact on our community; and to help foster a collective, political agenda for the lesbian and gay male community of greater Cincinnati.

We will report local news. We will pursue investigative reporting and analysis, and will endeavor to expose that gay news we find hidden in journalistic closets. We will tell you what city councils are doing; what police and courts are doing; what our own political leadership is doing. We will not publish a comprehensive list of resources, organizations and activities at this time, since this service is provided already. As much as seems prudent, we will not duplicate what is already being done.

Through a liberal use of editorials, readers' letters and guest columns, we will present a wide range of issues and viewpoints. We believe the dialogue will prove valuable to our people in forming their personal opinions, and to our community in finding a collective voice. We think this will encourage more political participation by greater numbers of lesbians and gay men. And we hope to be a catalyst through which together, we in the Queen City area will develop a tangible, political agenda for our collective future.

Finally, a few policy notes. The Gay Beat will appear on the first of every month (except, because of the Inaugural issue, for February 1985). Please submit letters, articles or advertisements by the 20th of the month before you want them to appear. Advertising rates will be made available on request. The editor reserves the right to include, in whole or in part, any material he or she receives, unless asked specifically not to do so. All material is copyrighted by The Gay Beat. Subscription rate is six dollars ($6) for twelve monthly issues, which will be mailed first-class in a plain envelope. Make check or money order payable to "The Gay Beat." Our mailing address is: THE GAY BEAT, P. O. Box 19124, CINCINNATI, OH 45219

The subscription list will be held in the strictest confidence. We do ask that all correspondence include a name and an address or phone number for verification or follow-up. This, too, may be withheld from publication upon request. The Gay Beat is published by a collective. This issue is edited by Ed Hicks & Jon Mesinger. G

xxxxxxxxxxxxxxxxxxxxxxxxxxxxxxxxxxxxxxxxxxxxxxxxxxxxxxxxxxxxxxxxxxxxxxxxxxxxxxxxxxxxxx

SUPPORT THE GAY BEAT

*The Gay Beat needs your support. Pick us up! Give us the once-over. If you like us, tell your friends. If you hate us, tell your friends that, too!
*Buy a subscription. It's just six bucks, which is less than you'd spend on lunch with a date.
*Send a letter. Submit an article. Volun-

TESTING (cont. from p.3)

Blood that shows positive on Hoxworth's test will be pulled and destroyed. Anyone who feels forced into donating blood because of employer or peer pressure is given a phone number to request their donation be pulled. Dr. Greenwalt has promised confidentiality.

Mitzel on the Monsters Within Our Community, Arts & Entertainment, p. 16

GAYBEAT

$1²⁵

Vol. 6 No. 2   Ohio's Gay Newspaper   February 1990

City of Cincinnati Seeks Gay Firefighters, Police
1985 Discrimination Case Leads to New Agreement to Advertise Job Openings

by Josh Thomas

CINCINNATI—The Fire Division is looking for a few good men and women, and it no longer cares — officially, at least — if they are Gay or Lesbian.

Fire officials have purchased a small ad in *Gaybeat* to publicize their upcoming exam for firefighter positions. (The ad appears on p. 9 of this issue.) Stonewall Cincinnati, a Gay/Lesbian human rights organization, had negotiated with Safety Department officials behind the scenes since last summer on a wide range of

Stonewall Cincinnati boardmember Ted Good, point man in negotiations with city Safety Dept.

Cincinnati Firefighters Union president Tom Donovan, asked for comment,

honest with you. We think they should hire the people that are best qualified for the job, in all aspects. I'd be interested to see how it's received, but we have no position. We want to have the most qualified people fighting fires."

In a related development, Gay activists are also providing sensitivity training to a new class of recruits at the Police Academy, a process underway here since 1980.

The city has no ordinance or administrative policy prohibiting discrimination based on sexual orientation in city hiring, but a 1985 decision by the Civil Service

Stonewall board member Ted Good told *Gaybeat* the Stonewall negotiations resulted from a 1985 discrimination complaint filed with Civil Service. Firefighter recruit Bev Ventura alleged that she was asked if she had ever engaged in homosexual relations during a routine polygraph examination. After she answered yes, the fire division made the training process impossible for her to pass, she claimed, and she was removed from the recruit class.

Ventura contacted Stonewall, and its then-president Richard Buchanan, a

The Gay *Nouveau*

50¢

APRIL '88

VOLUME I **GREATER CINCINNATI'S GAY NEWS JOURNAL** NUMBER I

'Gay' Ad to Appear in Phone Book

Businesswoman Credits First to Stonewall Cincinnati

by Ed Hicks

CINCINNATI—In a precedent-setting move, the publishers of the Yellow Pages will allow the words 'gay and lesbian' in a June, 1988 phone directory ad. The Reuben H. Donnelley company has a policy against the use of those words. Company officials backed down, though, after a local advertiser sought the help of Stonewall Cincinnati.

Dr. Irene Romanchuk submitted a display ad last January for the Ashland Psychological Group, using the term 'gay and lesbian issues' in the ad copy. Ashland had advertised in the Yellow Pages regularly, but had not referred to its gay practice before. The group discussed the change in copy "for about five minutes," Romanchuk told Nouveau, expecting it to be a routine matter.

"Our clerical person got the word Donnelley had refused the ad as it was, and would not use the words 'gay and lesbian,'" Romanchuk said. "They suggested the word 'homosexual' would be more appropriate, whereas "gay and lesbian' might be offensive to the general public." Romanchuk said the committee which reviews all ad copy was willing to consider "alternative terms."

"It sounds like discrimination," Romanchuk told Donnelley's Karen Lindquist. According to Romanchuk, Lindquist "evaded my questions" about the company's policy and the makeup of the review committee — except to say that she herself was a member of the committee, and that as far as she knew, the policy was also in effect in the company's Chicago office. "If you want to write to the committee you can write to me, and I will share it with them," Romanchuk said she was told.

"She had been so adamant when I talked to her on the phone I was convinced this was going to be a drawn-out battle." But Romanchuk refused to accept the term 'homosexual' because, she said, it sounded

clinical and negative to the people Ashland was trying to reach.

So Romanchuk spoke with John Maddux, chairman of Stonewall's Task Force on Discrimination. A letter of appeal was drafted to Donnelley. At the suggestion of attorney and Stonewall board member Richard Buchanan, a business notation was made at the bottom of the letter indicating a carbon copy to Stonewall. The appeal was submitted January 14. Meanwhile, Maddux planned a strategy for combatting Donnelley's anticipated rejection.

But the phone book publisher surprised everyone, notifying Ashland around the first of February that its appeal had been accepted and the ad would appear carrying the words 'gay and lesbian.'

'We need the community'

"It turned out to be awfully easy," Romanchuk said, "and I think Stonewall's involvement let them know they weren't dealing with just one queer."

"They haven't made a policy statement" though, Maddux said of the Donnelley company's decision. "But I'm confident this has set a precedent." He said the only similar case he knew of took place last year in Dade County, Florida – home of Anita Bryant's anti-gay crusade. That dispute, Maddux said, did lead to drawn-out court action.

Linquist told Nouveau, "I could not make any statements (about policy) on behalf of the company at this time." She said the issue was not the words 'gay' and 'lesbian' specifically, but "certain rules in general, geared to providing a directory of the highest integrity and value for everyone concerned." She would not elaborate on those rules. Lindquist expressed concern that "this thing not get blown out of proportion. These people are psychologists," she said, and "we allowed them to use the words."

"I'm usually pretty complacent," Romanchuk said. "Fifteen years ago I was a radical. At this point I'm out and comfortable and have found a lifestyle where I can be myself and not worry. This shook me out of my complacency, and made me glad there was a Stonewall. Even though I'm no longer vulnerable, we need a community. ▼

Gay Man Fired After Test Reported

Urges Anonymous HIV Testing

by Ed Hicks

CINCINNATI—A 38-year old gay man was fired from his job when his employer learned that he had taken the AIDS antibody test. Though he tested negative at that time, the man has since developed AIDS-related complex (ARC). He now advises others to "go to your public health department" for anonymous testing.

The gay man, "George," decided to take the HIV test because he was experiencing symptoms associated with AIDS, including night sweats and extreme fatigue. He said that sometimes he was so tired he could work no more than three half-days a week. He went for the test to his private physician because, he said, "I liked him and I trusted him." Though the test was negative it was reported on the insurance form, a copy of which went back to the company.

George worked four years for Brendamour Warehousing, Moving and Distribution Co. in Cincinnati, he said. He thought the people he worked with were his friends. His boss' secretary, a woman named Annette, had loaned him about $3,000 over a three-year period, George said – in exchange for being named beneficiary on his $20,000 life-insurance policy. George knew he was sick – he had had "constant lung infections" and had been in the hospital three times – but tried to make his boss and co-workers believe that he had cancer. "I thought I had to lie about my illness," George said. He did not want them to know what he already suspected. George said his ex-lover had developed AIDS, and had committed suicide.

The day George discovered he had ARC, his boss came unexpectedly to his door. "He pushed his way into my home and said, 'Start talking,'" George said. So George told Brendamour that he was gay and had tested positive for the AIDS virus. Brendamour said he would not tell the other employees, according to George. George saw "contempt in his eyes."

But Brendamour phoned his secretary immediately, and she came over to George's home, he said. The

Continued on page 2

In April 1988, a new publication entered the scene, aptly named *Nouveau*. The front cover did not acknowledge its launch, instead detailing a story about the phone book allowing the words "gay and lesbian" in an ad, alongside a story of a Cincinnati man who was fired from his job after it was reported that he was tested for HIV. On the inside cover, the new publication was explained. "With this first issue, greater Cincinnati meets *Nouveau*. The word itself means 'new'; but this magazine offers and gay and lesbian community something it has long valued: local news. *Nouveau* belongs to Cincinnati and Northern Kentucky. It will support our community, contribute to it, and grow with it." The presses stopped on *Nouveau* in 1996. (Both, Ohio Lesbian Archives.)

Blacks raising bucks, prestige 3 | **Tyner's Tunes** 9 | **Ron Buchanan: your fitness personality** 13

N O U V E A U

M I D W E S T

January 1992 $2

New bill points to mandatory AIDS testing

by BERTRAM A. WORKUM
Chief Staff Writer

A bill that would require all health care workers in Ohio to report HIV positive status — and which Cincinnati Health Commissioner Dr. Stanley Broadnax calls the first step toward mandatory AIDS testing for everyone — has passed the Ohio House with only one no vote.

The bill (House Bill 419), as

said she wasn't sure whether she had voted for it or not.

"I believe that when anyone has HIV (positive) status, someone should know," Ms. Rankin said. But "I don't think it should be publicized."

Betsy Gressler, president of Stonewall Cincinnati, said she believes Mallory, Rankin and many other state representatives were caught off guard by the bill's sudden appearance on the House's

into law.

In addition, the bill would people a false sense of safety in regards to AIDS, he said. "It might make people feel they don't have to use precautions" in sex, Bunge said.

The main chance to kill the bill, Bunge said, is that it contradicts guidelines issued in July by the Centers for Disease Control in Atlanta. Those guidelines suggested voluntary testing for HIV status, but emphasized the need for

treatment, including invasive procedures such as surgery.

In Cincinnati, Dr. Broadnax said any type of forced testing for HIV concerns him.

If HB 419 becomes law, "some health providers won't get the test, or won't report their status," Broadnax said.

Bertram A. Workum is Nouveau's chief staff writer, with 20 years' experience as a reporter for

To the Root(s) was a collectively run, nonprofit journal, published quarterly in the late 1980s. Their purpose was to provide an ongoing source of reflection, resource-sharing, organizational information, and social/political analysis for the Greater Cincinnati LGBTQ community. The content was distinctly more literary (poems, book reviews, historical analysis, and more) than a strict reporting of the LGBTQ happenings of the time. (Jeff Bixby.)

To the Root(s)

A KNOCK-DOWN DRAG-OUT OF RADICAL QUEER POLITIKS.

VOLUME 1 NUMBER 1   SUMMER 1988 $2.00

A CINCINNATI

HOMOCENTENNIAL....

REMEMBERING OUR ROOTS

ACT-UP
C I N C I N N A T I

FEBRUARY/MARCH 1991

"WOMYN DON'T GET AIDS, THEY JUST DIE FROM IT"

On Dec. 3, 1990, ACT-UP/CINTI were in Atlanta for a demonstration at the Centers for Disease Control in conjunction with World AIDS Day. The focus was on Womyn and AIDS. The CDC does not include opportunistic infections that womyn develop differently from men on their list of diseases that when combined with HIV would result in a CDC-defined AIDS diagnosis. This keeps womyn out of clinical trials, and means that they often die shortly after they've been diagnosed, if at all.

Three members of the ACT-UP/CINTI Womyn's Caucus joined with the womyn's affinity group The Outside Educators. The band of about forty womyn invaded the campus of Emory University for some impromptu teach-ins. Classes were interrupted so that womyn with AIDS could share their experiences while leaflets about the CDC's ritual exclusion of womyn from studies were distributed to students. The womyn made their way across campus in the pouring rain amid chants of "AIDS is a disaster, Womyn

die faster," and "Womyn with AIDS can't wait till later. We're not your fucking incubator!" At one point they descended upon the cafeteria, and after a general mass of chants and bull-horn testamonies, they spent some time talking one-on-one with students and urged them to join the

WOMEN ARE DYING

FOR AIDS TREATMENT

demonstration in from of the CDC. After a temporary relief from the rain, the womyn set out again, this time with the campus policy in pursuit. Making their way through campus streets they met up with the rest of the demonstrators, turned and led the procession back through to the CDC.

For over two hours the demonstrators went about their business relatively hassle-free from the Dekalb County police that were on hand. Banners hung from trees, and the building was covered with stickers and slogans. Various affinity groups did theatrics while a picket line continued. By 2 o'clock the police began making arrests in particularly violent clashes with protestors, many of whom were either dragged away by arms and legs, or who were carried off between officers. Confusion abounded as marshalls struggled to keep the crowd back, and police often literally just grabbed bodies at random from the front lines. The crowd had already begun to shrink in numbers when police brought in wire-cutters to release the Chain Gang whose members had chained themselves to the front of the building. Finally,

See "Atlanta Action" pg. 2

ACT-UP IS A DIVERSE, NON-PARTISAN GROUP UNITED IN ANGER AND COMMITTED TO DIRECT ACTION TO END THE AIDS CRISIS.

As HIV/AIDS continued to decimate the gay community, ACT UP harnessed the power of print in order to more effectively convey their message, raise awareness, and organize for future actions. ACT UP Cincinnati launched a newsletter as a means to express their voice through a different medium, using ink as yet another opportunity to remind the community that silence equals death. (Ohio Lesbian Archives.)

GLUE

Gays and Lesbians United for Education

Vol. 1 No. 1   PO Box 19856 Cincinnati, Ohio 45219   Spring 1990

LESBIAN/GAY YOUTH WORKSHOPS

Last fall an agreement was reached with Cincinnati Public Schools Superintendent Dr. Lee Etta Powel allowing a group of professionals to provide inservice training on lesbian and gay youth issues to all CPS guidance counselors. This followed Dr. Powel's veto of a decision by the Core Design Team (a joint teacher-administration panel) to allow a gay/lesbian workshop to be presented at the annual Education Convention.

CPS High School Head Counselors received training in February, the Elementary Counselors in March, and the Jr. High Counselors will receive training shortly in April.

—See "Workshops", page 2

GLUE ELECTS OFFICERS

At a lively dinner meeting in G.J.'s Gaslight, Jan Lenz and Dan Stephen were elected co-chairs of GLUE for the next year. Jeff Bixby was elected Treasurer and Bob Zimmerman Secretary. Barron Wilson agreed to serve as Anti-Discrimination Committee Chair, Ruth Rowan and Tris Gibson will head the Social

—See "Officers", page 2

ANN NORTHRUP TO VISIT

Ann Northrup, Educational Outreach Chair of the Hetrick-Martin Institute for the Protection of Lesbian and Gay Youth (New York City) will be a keynote speaker at this year's Lesbian and Gay Pride Day parade and rally downtown (Saturday June 9 11:00 at Fountain Square). Her visit is sponsored jointly by GLUE and the Greater Cincinnati Lesbian/Gay Coalition. Ms. Northrup is a leading figure in the movement for lesbian/gay youth. She has met with local school boards in the New York area to do training on lesbian/gay youth and AIDS. In addition, Ms. Northrup has done inservice training to a wide number of groups nationally. She is a permanent member of ACT-UP (AIDS Coalition to Unleash Power) New York and helps facilitate many of their weekly meetings. Before her involvement with Hetrick-Martin, Ms. Northrup was a producer for CBS News.

GLUE members can meet Ms. Northrup at a pre-parade cocktail party the evening of June 8. Tickets are $20 or whatever you can afford and will help defray the costs of this year's Pride Week events. For time and location of this event, or to buy tickets, call Jeff Bixby at 871-3892.

The first newsletter for Gays and Lesbians United for Education (GLUE) was sent out in Spring 1990, barely a year after the group first formed. In addition to listings for social networking and professional development opportunities, the first newsletter also featured an announcement that GLUE would be reviewing the policy for Cincinnati Public Schools that granted the Superintendent the authority to decide whether an employee could keep their teaching assignment if they were found to have AIDS. Subsequent years of GLUE newsletters offered the same type of content: a crucial mix of opportunities for teachers to gather and advocacy to scaffold their day-to-day lives in education. (Both, Jeff Bixby.)

Gays and Lesbians United for Education

Fall 1992

Welcome Back!!

Greetings to all supporters of GLUE! After an end-of-the-year hiatus and the long damp summer we're back with some change in format. We're still working on learning to execute this publication with the same high quality as Dan Stephen produced, but please be patient until such time as we figure out desk-top publishing.

As you know, it has been an eventful summer, the political season heating up with "family values" issue, locally, the hearings on the Human Rights Ordinance. These seem to be great and terrible times for the lesbian and gay community. Educators are targeted specifically by the religious right, if one is to go on the testimony of the

opponents of the ordinance. Responsible, dedicated men and women in the classroom are the worst nightmare of the radical, religious right. Because we are trustworthy, caring and principled, we show up the "Big Lie" about all gays and lesbians for what it is. As Kirk and Madsen say in *After the Ball*:"... straights are afraid that gay teachers will stand as living refutations of society's worst myths about homosexuals; this might soften homohatred in the next generation and enable gay children to come out earlier and better adjusted, with less shame and self-hatred."

Ed Hausfeld

Fun Up There

"I'M A LESBIAN, I'M A TEACHER AND I'M PROUD!!" This was the cheer we gave for ourselves as about 40 women gathered at the Michigan Womyn's Music Festival August 11 for an all-day workshop called "Making Ourselves Whole as Lesbian Teachers." On that chilly morning we sat under big trees and shared our situations, where we taught, how "out" we are in our schools and what problems we are having. We then identified many positive characteristics of a lesbian teacher. Some of the characteristics are: we are good role models, we are dedicated, we are sensitive and diverse. We are catalysts for change, stereotype-breakers, risk-takers and we are empathetic toward others. And from the standpoint of the district that hires us, we are cost effective, since we generally do not have kids of our own.

We did some other activities during the day, but the topic that interested me the most was building allies in our schools. An ally is a friends who is not lesbian or gay but who is willing to stick her neck out without being afraid of homophobic repercussions. She (or he) is someone who speaks up and

See **Fun**, p. 2

GLUE   PO Box 19856, Cincinnati, Ohio 45219   542-5599 or 242-2491

EDITORIAL PAGE

TUESDAY, JUNE 12, 2001

In a sobering reminder that the stigma surrounding HIV/AIDS still saturated society, the *Cincinnati Enquirer* ran an editorial cartoon on June 12, 2001—the anniversary of the AIDS epidemic—that evoked the shame and victim-blaming mentality of the 1980s and 1990s. As Kathleen Cox, president of the board of directors of Caracole, wrote in a published letter-to-the-editor, the cartoon "serves only to shame and further stigmatize those HIV infected and affected." She further highlighted the reality that Cincinnati had for years been a city "torn apart by stereotypes and misunderstanding," advocating instead for a compassionate approach that "would go a long way toward addressing and healing the challenges facing our city." (Both, Caracole.)

AIDS cartoon offers inaccuracy, meanness

The board of directors of Caracole Inc. was shocked and saddened by the June 12 cartoon by syndicated cartoonist Michael Ramirez [grim reaper] that recognized the anniversary of the AIDS epidemic.

Not only is the cartoon factually inaccurate, but the sentiment is mean-spirited and serves only to shame and further stigmatize those HIV infected and affected.

Syndicated cartoonist Michael Ramirez plays on the ignorance and fear we have been fighting since the 1980s and promotes a blame-the-victim mentality about a serious and incurable disease.

In a city torn apart by stereotypes and misunderstanding, this is an example of a missed opportunity to educate our community and convey a spirit of support.

It also was a missed opportunity to mark the great advances in both treatment and prevention programs over the two decades.

Such a compassionate approach would go a long way toward addressing and healing the challenges facing our city.

— **Kathleen Cox**
President, Board of Directors
of Caracole Inc.

59

THE CRAZY LADIES BOOKSTORE

THE CRAZY LADIES BOOKSTORE NEWSLETTER
November/December, 1987

* * * * * * * * * * *

As the Holiday Season approaches (and the Ludlow Viaduct is open this year) we are beginning to fill the shelves with new books, calendars, music, cards, and other items for you to give to those you love. We have had a very busy September and October. Author Katherine Forrest was at the store on the 19th and we had our biggest sales day ever! In September we sold books at a Procter and Gamble Workshop for Women Managers at Marriot. We met and sold to women from all over the country.

That was good training for our big event in October, the Women-Church Convergence. We had a great location for our booth and an efficient good-looking shelving display unit designed and made for us by Deborah Winters. These pluses combined with many hours of hard work by Joan Schell, Maureen Wood, Jo Wolf and other women helped us to sell an incredible number of books, tapes, buttons and cards in 2-1/2 days. Charlotte Bunch stopped by to autograph copies of her new book, Passionate Politics and Gloria Steinem came to our booth and bought some books. Both liked the name of our store and it was fun to meet and talk with them both.

The Crazy Ladies Collective wishes you all a happy, fulfilling holiday season and new year. Thanks to all the volunteers and staff for our best year ever at the Bookstore. Thanks to you, our customers for continuing to support your women's bookstore.

Please join us for our Holiday Reception on Saturday, December 19th from 2:00 until 5:00 p.m. Enjoy a hot drink and some good food while you do your last minute shopping.

* * * * * * * * * * *

HOLIDAY HOURS: We are open everyday and will be open on Monday nights in December until 8:00, as well as Thursdays until 8:00 p.m.

We will close at 5:00 on Thursday, December 24 and Thursday, December 31. We will be closed Christmas Day and New Year's Day.

4112 Hamilton Ave.   Cincinnati, OH 45223   (513) 541-4198

It was not just organizations that put out newsletters to connect with the LGBTQ community in Cincinnati; local businesses got in on the publication action too. Long before social media provided an easy outlet to announce a sale, trumpet an event, or even announce holiday hours, business owners needed to use every mode of communication at their disposal to engage potential customers. Whether it was Crazy Ladies Bookstore heralding either the arrival of new literature or the impending visit of a feminist poet, or Spurs Cincinnati mailing out their newsletter (*The Rowel*) that introduced Barracks Night, Movie Night, continental brunch, and wished a happy birthday to customers by their first name and membership number, business newsletters were a key ingredient to creating customers who were in the know. (Left, Ohio Lesbian Archives; below, Jeff Bixby.)

326 EAST EIGHTH STREET
CINCINNATI, OHIO 45202
(513) 721-9007

MAY 1984   THE ROWEL   Vol. II No. 5

APRIL may have been all showers, but spring has finally sprung. SPURS ended the month by announcing something new, Cincinnati Coast to Coast. It's a continental brunch offered between 1 and 4 pm on Sundays. Along with bagels and cream cheese, danish and coffee, we offer Bloody Bulls juice drinks and California OJ (orange juice and champagne) for one low price. Come down and join us early on Sundays and see SPURS in a different light.

Money made the world go around the weekend of April 13th. Our Sleaze Friday turned into 1040 SLE-Z and the Bankers party on Saturday brought out the suits. Did anyone recognize Dale in his pinstripes? The full moon fell on the 15th this month and our customers showed how the IRS really can take the shirt right off your back. April was only the beginning. Get into the spirit and swing into spring.

YOU ASKED FOR IT SPURS does listen to its customers. Because of many requests, we are going to bring you some oldies but goodies on Movie Night. Come and see Mildred Pierce or Blanche in What Ever Happened to Baby Jane?

UNCLE SAM WANTS YOU and so does SPURS the night of Saturday the 19th when the bar becomes a barracks at Fort Dicks. Wear your uniforms but don't't worry if you can't find one, we'll be inducting everyone into one of the four branches of service. See you in the barracks!

RACING FANS TAKE NOTE. May is the month of races with the Kentucky Derby and the Indy 500 taking place. Avoid the hassle of crowds and driving and join us at SPURS. We'll be showing both on the widescreen. We also will throw our own celebrations with a Post Derby Party on the 6th, and an Indy 500 Party on Sunday the 27th.

MARK YOUR CALENDAR June 30th is the date and the place to be is Sharon Woods for SPURS annual picnic. There will be dancing and beer and metts and volleyball and beer and softball and men and more beer, well you get the idea. Just be careful of any bears in the Woods! More information will be coming.

HAPPY BIRTHDAYS are becoming a regular part of TADS on Tuesdays. If you would like to celebrate yours or someone else's then let the bartenders know, and we'll provide the cake. Speaking of which, Happy Birthdays to Charlie#26, Carl#50, Stan#53, Kenny#69, Hal#83, Earl#88, Ron#116, David#117, Bob#125, Jim#130, Kim#133, Ron#135, Jim#143, Dan#165, Larry#190, David#191, Ernie#205, Wally#210, Chuck#254, James#266.

Don't forget, if you would like to receive THE ROWEL and our monthly schedule by mail in a plain envelope, fill out the info below and leave it at SPURS or mail it to us.

NAME
STREET, NUMBER, APT. ETC.
CITY, STATE, ZIP

Four

WE ORGANIZE

ACTIVISM AND ISSUES

Whether responding to national events or phenomena that were distinctly more Cincinnatian, the LGBTQ community banded together countless times over the years to protest a discriminatory action, to draw attention to a lack of equality, and to demand change when rights were at stake. When the inspired speech, the creative sign, or the well-crafted letter was needed, Cincinnati has never experienced a shortage of impassioned and brave voices ready to be heard. (Jeff Bixby.)

THE HISTORY OF ISSUE 3

1982: Stonewall Cincinnati is formed. Its mission is to end discrimination against all people, especially against those who face discrimination based on sexual orientation.

1991: Stonewall successfully lobbies Cincinnati City Council to add sexual orientation to the anti-discrimination language of its EEO policies.

1992: Ten years after it is founded, Stonewall Cincinnati leads the efforts to assure passage of the Human Rights Ordinance by Cincinnati City Council making it illegal to discriminate on the basis of race, gender, religion, marital status, age, disability status, HIV status, sexual orientation, national and ethnic origin and Appalachian regional origin.

1993: By a 68% margin voters pass Issue 3 which prohibits the City from enforcing the protections of the Human Rights Ordinance for gay men, lesbians and bisexuals.

1993: U.S. District Judge S. Arthur Spiegel finds that Issue 3 is unconstitutional and issues a permanent injunction.

1994: Cincinnati City Council votes to join our opposition in appealing Judge Spiegel's decision.

1994: U.S. Court of Appeals for the 6th District reverses Judge Spiegel's findings allowing Issue 3 to be implemented.

1994: City Councilmember Dwight Tillery, citing the 1993 ballot results and the Court of Appeals ruling reverses his support and becomes the decisive fifth vote to remove sexual orientation from the Human Rights Ordinance.

1996: The U.S. Supreme Court strikes down Colorado's Amendment 2 which uses the same language as Cincinnati's Issue 3.

1996: The U.S. Supreme Court instructs the U.S. Court of Appeals for the 6th District to reconsider their findings on Issue 3 in light of the Supreme Court's ruling on Amendment 2.

1997: The U.S. Court of Appeals for the 6th District hears arguments from both sides before reconsidering their earlier findings. Their decision my be released at any time.

A favorable decision by the 6th District Court would pave the way for efforts to once again add sexual orientation to the Human Rights Ordinance.

An unfavorable decision would lead to another appeal to the U.S. Supreme Court.

In 1987, LGBTQ people gathered from all over the world to participate in the Second National March on Washington for Lesbian and Gay Rights, often referred to as the "the Great March" due to both sheer number of the assembled participants as well as its critical timing of the event coinciding with the inescapable decimation of HIV/AIDS. The almost-week-long array of activities included a protest in front of the IRS, a sit-in on the steps of the Supreme Court to protest *Bowers v. Hardwick* (with police officers, many wearing rubber gloves, arresting more than 600 LGBTQ activists), and the first public display of the AIDS Memorial Quilt. Cincinnati was well represented at the March, traveling together to represent their city and Ohio amongst the masses even as they stood side-by-side with their LGBTQ siblings from every corner of the globe fighting to have their voices heard. (Above, Scott Knox; below, Jeff Bixby.)

The NAMES Project AIDS Memorial Quilt came to the Cincinnati Convention Center from March 24–26, 1989, giving visitors the opportunity to bear witness to a visible display of the devastation that AIDS wrought on our community. Legendary activist Cleve Jones organized the creation of the Quilt in 1985 as a memorial for those who had died of AIDS. He called it "a statement of hope and remembrance, a symbol of national unity, and a promise of love." The Quilt was seen as a stark contrast to the more direct strategies employed by groups such as ACT UP. The last display of the full Quilt in 1996 covered the entire National Mall in Washington, DC. (Both, Jeff Bixby.)

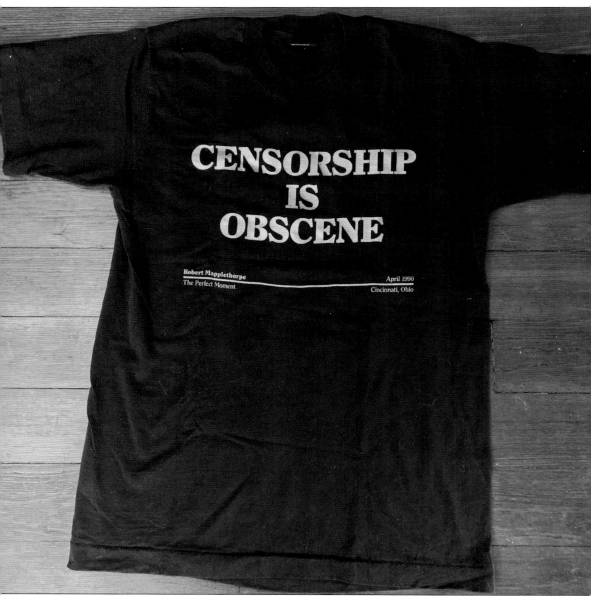

In 1990, the Contemporary Arts Center (CAC) hosted "The Perfect Moment," a collection of 175 photographs by Robert Mapplethorpe. Anticipating controversy, CAC director Dennis Barrie went to court and attempted to have the exhibit declared not obscene. The court refused, and law enforcement officials entered the arts center on the exhibition's opening day to indict CAC and Barrie for criminal violations of the Ohio obscenity statute. The case quickly attracted national attention as the very question of "What is art?" was being asked, as was whether tax dollars—via the National Endowment for the Arts—should be used to finance "questionable" material. Impassioned protests followed as anti-censorship advocates squared off against those claiming some of the photographs only appealed to prurient interests. Seven months later, a jury found CAC and Barrie not guilty of the charges, convinced by the army of defense witnesses who testified that Mapplethorpe's work was serious and brilliant art. (Jeff Bixby.)

On September 3, 1991, Steven O'Banion was arrested for jaywalking and disorderly conduct. He was charged with attempted murder and felonious assault (carrying a sentence of up to 125 years in prison) after corrections officers and a jail nurse claimed the O'Banion, a man living with AIDS, spit blood and saliva on them. O'Banion testified that he was punched four times in the face by officers as they hurled antigay words at him, and his assaulters came into contact with his blood after he was beaten up. The trial featured experts who had to explain that HIV could not be transmitted via surface-level exposure. The judge dismissed the attempted murder charges and ultimately sentenced O'Banion to 20 days in the same jail where the assault occurred. LGBTQ activists, led by Gay and Lesbian March Activists and ACT UP, came together for a rally at the Hamilton County Justice Center to have the charges dropped and demand the resignation of Sheriff Leis, whom they accused of harassing the gay community. (Ohio Lesbian Archives.)

If the 1987 march was "great," then the 1993 event was even "greater." With estimates as high as one million participants, the 1993 March on Washington for Lesbian, Gay, and Bi Equal Rights and Liberation stands today as one of the largest protests in the history of the United States. The demands of the event were multiple and varied, including passage of an LGBTQ civil rights bill, repeal of sodomy laws, a massive increase in HIV/AIDS-related funding, and an end to sexist, racial, and ethnic discrimination. The event was notable not only for its size and scope but also for having bisexual people included in the title of the event. Once again, Cincinnati was well represented. The Greater Cincinnati Gay and Lesbian Coalition brought together myriad organizations and individuals from across the Queen City to link arms and march as one. (Above Ron Clemons; left, Jeff Bixby.)

In November 1992, the Cincinnati City Council passed an ordinance that "prohibited discrimination in employment, housing or accommodation because of sexual orientation." The Citizens for Community Values reared their heads, mobilizing to place Issue 3 on the 1993 ballot, which would repeal the language and enshrine the discriminatory language as an amendment to the city's charter. Those seeking to defeat Issue 3 attempted to oppose its passage through events and individual voter engagement but were hampered by an advertising/marketing strategy that did not resonate with the citizenry. Issue 3 was approved by a landslide, 56,416 to 34,472. A lengthy court battle ensued: a US district judge struck the charter amendment down as unconstitutional, the Sixth Circuit Court of Appeals overturned this ruling, and the Supreme Court refused to review the case, resulting in the discriminatory language standing for more than a decade. (Both, Ohio Lesbian Archives.)

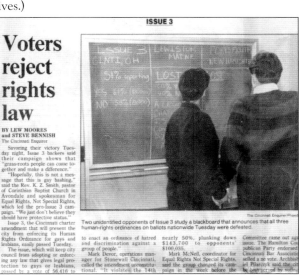

ISSUE 3

Voters reject rights law

BY LEW MOORES
and STEVE BENNISH
The Cincinnati Enquirer

Savoring their victory Tuesday night, Issue 3 backers said their campaign shows that "grass-roots people can come together and make a difference."

"Hopefully, this is not a message that this is gay bashing," said the Rev. K. Z. Smith, pastor of Corinthian Baptist Church in Avondale and spokesman for Equal Rights, Not Special Rights, which led the pro-Issue 3 campaign. "We just don't believe they should have protective status."

Issue 3, the Cincinnati charter amendment that will prevent the city from enforcing its Human Rights Ordinance for gays and lesbians, easily passed Tuesday.

The issue, which will keep city council from adopting or enforcing any law that gives legal protection to gays or lesbians, passed by a vote of 56,416 to

to enact an ordinance of hatred and discrimination against a group of people."

Mark Dever, operations manager for Stonewall Cincinnati, called the amendment unconstitutional. "It violates the 14th

nearly 50%, plunking down $143,700 to opponents' $100,035.

Mark McNeil, coordinator for Equal Rights Not Special Rights, said the group changed its campaign in the week before the

Committee came out against Issue. The Hamilton County Republican Party endorsed a no vote. The Cincinnati Bar Association voted a no vote. Archbishop Daniel Pilarczyk said the city would be best served by voting

Two unidentified opponents of Issue 3 study a blackboard that announces that all three human-rights ordinances on ballots nationwide Tuesday were defeated.

Cincinnati has been home to both LGBTQ buycotts and boycotts—two very different initiatives. In June 1995, the Buycott Project was launched in an effort to help raise awareness of human rights. Volunteers went to local businesses and providers and asked them to complete cards indicating their level of diversity awareness and commitment, with supporters being listed in a special booklet. Key to the success of this action was that the cards asked about more than a commitment to LGBTQ customers and more broadly included other categories of underrepresented populations. In March 2002, Stonewall Cincinnati signed onto "the Boycott": an action sponsored by the Coalition for a Just Cincinnati that called for an economic boycott of downtown until a set of demands were met including accountability in the Cincinnati Police Department, economic inclusion of people of color, and the repeal of Article XII. Stonewall Cincinnati's decision to be a part of the boycott was not without vociferous opposition, particularly as participation meant working with some of the very same ministers who championed Article XII. (Both, Jeff Bixby.)

After a decade of Cincinnati relegating the LGBTQ community to second class citizenship after the passage of Article XII, signs of progress finally started to appear. A study by the National Conference for Community and Justice indicated that attitudes towards the LGBTQ community had become more favorable. Several large corporations like Federated Department Stores and Procter & Gamble added sexual orientation to their nondiscrimination policies. There was strong support for an LGBTQ-inclusive human rights ordinance in nearby Covington, Kentucky. Numerous studies indicated that there was a real and true economic loss to the city due to the discriminatory language. All of this positive movement culminated in 2003 when the Cincinnati City Council overwhelmingly passed an inclusive hate crimes ordinance. The time finally felt right to address the blight on Cincinnati's charter, and the Citizens to Restore Fairness held a press conference at the Underground Railroad Freedom Center to launch the campaign to repeal Article XII. (Terry Payne.)

The first step in the repeal process of Article XII was to get the initiative on the ballot. To do so, 6771 signatures were needed. The Citizens to Restore Fairness (CRF) were aiming for 12,000 to account for errors, such as people who signed the petition who were not registered to vote. The drive to collect signatures was launched on April 26, 2003, at the Ohio Valley GLBT Power Summit, where the first 280 signatures were collected. The gathering of signatures also created the first opportunities to connect with voters. Research had shown that voters did not fully understand what they were passing in 1993, and there was little time back then to organize opposition. With well over a year until the 2004 election, CRF was ready to educate the populace with time to spare. Over 13,000 signatures were submitted, and the initiative was certified to be placed on the ballot. Eleven years later, the language would again be listed as Issue 3, but this time a "Yes" vote would *restore* fairness. (Terry Payne.)

One of the key strategies in repealing Article XII was outreach to communities of color. For years, there had been a narrative that there was little support within that population for their LGBTQ siblings, so special attention was paid to highlight that there was a direct correlation between the racism and hate speech directed at communities of color and the stereotypes and hate speech hurled at the LGBTQ community. This outreach yielded tremendous support. (Terry Payne.)

The goal to repeal Article XII was simple, if overwhelming in scope: to have one-on-one conversations with each of the 360,000-plus citizens in all 52 communities in Hamilton County. To accomplish this feat, trained volunteers were needed. There were multiple opportunities for individuals to learn more about the history of the legislation and how to hit the key points of repeal before setting out into the world to change one mind at a time. (Terry Payne.)

SCOTT E. KNOX
Attorney at Law

Street, Suite 300
o 45202

(513) 241-3800
Facsimile (513) 241-4032
e-mail: sknox@choice.net

hand-delivered

March 8, 2002

Hon. Steve Chabot
3003 Carew Tower
441 Vine Street
Cincinnati, Ohio 45202

Dear Representative Chabot:

I am writing to let you know in my experience as an attorney how often I become aware of an instance of discrimination against a person due to his or her perceived sexual orientation, either in the workplace or in housing.

As you know, sometimes the people get lost in the statistics, so I wanted to include a description of two incidents that are fairly typical. I spoke with a man, "John" who said that his supervisor (at a large restaurant chain) found out that John was gay and began referring to him as "that fag". This affected John's working relationships with co-workers and people that he supervised, as it gave the message that he was 'less than' the others, and therefore deserving of less respect. He complained to the chain's district manager, who seemed sympathetic, but then promoted John's supervisor. John called me because he overheard his new supervisor asking, "I need John here - where is that fag?". John was very upset when I talked to him, to the point that he did not want to return to work even though he had enjoyed his job a great deal. He was certain that he must have some legal recourse, as would an African American if his supervisor referred to him as "that nigger" or a Jewish person if he were referred to as "that kike".

Unfortunately, I had to tell him that his only recourse, besides complaining to the same system that promoted the previous perpetrator, was to quit and file for unemployment, hoping that the unemployment adjudicator would agree that degrading him until he left was tantamount to firing him without just cause. He could then, at least, collect unemployment while looking for another job. I'm not sure what he could tell the next employer as to the reason he left his previous job.

Last week I spoke with a bright mental health professional, "Paul" who had provided information to me for a SSI claim I was handling. We got talking and he told me that he had previously worked for an employer where he was doing a great job, was well-respected, and where he felt he would stay until he retired. Paul then heard two of his supervisors saying how glad they were that no 'fags' worked there. He knew at that point that if his employer found out he was gay his job would not be secure. Paul left that job and found one for far less money and less potential for growth, as well as losing a substantial pension benefit. His employer never knew why he left.

Just as with most of this type of case, neither of these employees would appear on any 'anti-gay discrimination' radar screen. However in my practice I see such instances regularly. Approximately fifteen to twenty times a year I get a call from a potential client stating that he or

The attempts to appeal Article XII came, by necessity, in so many different forms. In addition to the person-to-person conversations, the appeal to elected officials, and the public rallies of support, many in the legal community lent their voices to the cause to demonstrate the effects of the charter amendment. In this example, attorney Scott Knox wrote a letter to Rep. Steve Chabot to explain that Knox saw cases of workplace and housing discrimination based on sexual orientation with great regularity. Knox then went on to prove a negative: clearly laying out that "due to societal pressures, most people who suffer from such discrimination do not want to publicly claim they are gay" while other LGBTQ people in Cincinnati would know about Article XII and would hence also not come forward. Thus, Knox made the case that the number of complaints he received actually represented a far larger number of individuals negatively harmed by the discriminatory language. (Both, Scott Knox.)

she has suffered some adverse employment action due to his or her actual or perceived sexual orientation. Most often this takes the form of harassment (something over half of the calls), with the rest being complaints of lack of promotion or termination. A few, perhaps one or two a year, seem spurious on their face, as where someone has a terrible attendance record that could easily account for the disciplinary action.

It is important to remember that:

(1) I'm not the only attorney that local people would come to with such complaints,
(2) due to societal pressures, most people who suffer from such discrimination do not want to publicly claim they are gay, so would never call an attorney to dispute the adverse action,
(3) it is likely that most gay people in the Cincinnati area must know that under Cincinnati's City Charter Article XII, there can be no laws protecting them anyway (or they call the Civil Rights Commission, the EEOC, or a friend and find this out), so they decide that it is futile to call an attorney.

Using thirteen arguably valid complaints coming to me a year, if I get even one in five who go to an attorney, that's a minimum of 65 complaints a year that go to attorneys. If one-third of the victims are 'out' enough to complain (surely an over-estimate), the true number of events becomes 195. If even half of the people in this area know that it is futile to seek action due to the Charter amendment, this number becomes 390 instances of employment discrimination based on perceived or actual sexual orientation each year, as a minimum figure.

I do not get as many complaints of housing discrimination based on sexual orientation, perhaps five or six a year. I think similar factors apply to that number, so it, too, is a small portion of the actual incidents of discrimination.

I hope you can join the effort to change this situation, as it is not good for the victims of this discrimination nor for our businesses, which lose good workers, nor for our community, which (beyond the ethical problems) ends up with qualified workers unemployed or leaving the area.

Respectfully,

Scott Knox

It would be a colossal understatement to say that tensions were running high during the fight to repeal Article XII. Ten years can really change a city, and the period of time between 1993 and 2004 was no exception in Cincinnati. There were many and different camps: those who were present when Issue 3 originally passed, those who had moved to Cincinnati in the intervening years, those who wanted a radical approach to activism, those who wanted to be more palatable, and those who represented everyone in between. Though the common goal was a victory for LGBTQ equality, the route to actually reach that end was much disputed. Stonewall Cincinnati became a focal point for many peoples' frustration as there was a sense in some parts of the community that Stonewall was not living up to (perhaps the impossibly high) expectations associated with being the oldest standing LGBTQ advocacy organization in the city. (Both, Ron Clemons.)

YES! FOR FAIRNESS

Repeal Article XII

Volunteer

In 2004, Cincinnati voters repealed Article XII by 54 percent to 46 percent. It was an extraordinary victory, particularly given the context of that year's election in which 13 states banned same-sex marriage. Ohio was one of those states. Remarkably, the repeal of Article XII was the only ballot victory for the LGBTQ community in the entire country that year. By all accounts, the victory would not have been achieved without the actions of the volunteers. As Justin Turner, the campaign manager for Citizens to Restore Fairness, wrote to the volunteers shortly after the election, "Our historic victory would not have been possible without your commitment. Your involvement in this campaign has been an inspiration." The victory led to the formation of Equality Cincinnati, which later became part of Equality Ohio. In 2006, by a margin of 8-1, the Cincinnati City Council passed a human rights ordinance offering employment and housing protections to the LGBTQ community. It was similar to the legislation passed in 1992 but with one major difference: these protections were left standing. (Terry Payne.)

Over 300 students at Miami University and the University of Cincinnati held coinciding rallies on April 6, 2012, in response to a brutal hate crime. On March 24, two students (representing the two institutions) were attacked while holding hands and walking home from an LGBTQ event. The attackers screamed antigay slurs before violently beating the two students, leaving them bloody and battered. The "Miami & UC Unite Against Hate!" emergency action rally created the opportunity for the two schools to stand united in their demand for safe places to live, learn, work, and show affection. The rallies featured intersectional signs highlighting that hate should not be tolerated whether based on race, ethnicity, sexual orientation, gender identity/expression, disability, or any other classification. (Both, Michael Chanak Jr.)

Leelah Alcorn Vigil

Program &
Resource Guide

Saturday, Janurary 10th.

Woodward Theater
1404 Main Street
Cincinnati, OH

The Greater Cincinnati area and the global LGBTQ community were hit hard with the news on December 28, 2014, that 17-year-old Leelah Alcorn died by suicide on a highway in her hometown of Kings Mills, roughly 25 miles northeast of Cincinnati. Leelah's parents refused to accept her gender identity and sent her to Christian-based conversion therapy. In her suicide note, she wrote, "The only way I will rest in peace is if one day transgender people aren't treated the way I was, they're treated like humans, with valid feelings and human rights. . . . My death needs to mean something." Councilman Chris Seelbach shared her note on social media, which quickly resulted in worldwide attention and helped increase awareness about the plight of many trans youth. In November 2015, the interchange of Interstate 71 South and Ohio State Route 48 was dedicated to her memory, and the Ohio Department of Transportation unveiled signs reading, "In Memory of Leelah Alcorn" along that stretch of road. The following month, Cincinnati became the second US city to ban conversion therapy. (Left, Ohio Lesbian Archives; below, Sydney Spata.)

Representation matters. When openly LGBTQ individuals step up and run for public office, they do so knowing that they will face a type of scrutiny that their heterosexual opponents simply will not face. Though there has been any number of candidates and officeholders in Cincinnati who were "known" to be LGBTQ but not actually out, the past decade has seen an influx of those choosing to run from outside the closet. In 2011, Chris Seelbach made history when he was elected as the first openly gay politician to the Cincinnati City Council, championing myriad LGBTQ equality issues over the years. Tamaya Dennard was elected to city council in 2017 and became the first openly gay woman of color elected to public office in the city. She was famously sworn in holding a folding chair, fond of Congresswoman Shirley Chisholm's quote: "If they don't give you a seat at the table, bring a folding chair." (Above, Chris Seelbach; below, *Prizm*.)

What happens when the love that dares not speak its name decides instead to shout it from the rooftops for all the world to hear? Legalizing same-sex marriage was a focus of the LGBTQ community for so long that, when the Supreme Court made equality the law of the land in 2015, the rejoicing could be heard in every corner of the country, most certainly including Cincinnati. Still, with the LGBTQ community in Ohio still lacking protections in housing, employment, and public accommodations, equality has not been achieved. Protests, rallies, and writing letters can be effective modes of creating change. But so too is dropping to one knee in front of a crowd at a roller derby or an audience at a drag show and proposing to the one you love, telling everyone around you, "My love is every bit as strong as yours." Bonus points if the other person says, "Yes." (Left, Jason Bechtel; below, JAC Stringer.)

Five

WE MARCH
PRIDE CELEBRATIONS

Let it always be remembered: the first major Pride held in Ohio was celebrated in Cincinnati. Before their siblings in Cleveland and Columbus came together in their respective cities, a small but powerful group gathered together in Washington Park in 1973 to set the tone for decades to come: LGBTQ neighbors standing shoulder-to-shoulder in authenticity, celebration, and, yes, pride. (Jeff Bixby.)

Independent Eye

MAY, 1973   ISSUE: VOLUME 6, NUMBER 2

Ohio Newsreel Hassled

In the middle of March, there was an unsuccessful arson attempt at the building where Newsreel has its offices. The source of the attempt is still unknown. On March 30th, after leaving the office for the day, federal treasury agents broke into our office with a search warrant, messed up the office, looked through the files, and confiscated one Vietnamese and three Cuban films. Legal proceedings for the return of the films have been started. This is not the only Newsreel to meet with problems: Los Angeles Newsreel has been firebombed at least five times, New York Newsreel has been hassled and harrassed by treasury department and customs officials, and members of San Francisco Newsreel have been subpoened to Grand Juries for their films.

Newsreel is an international group of filmmakers and distributors which started in 1967. The members of Newsreel, however, are more than just filmmakers, they are activists dedicated to making changes in this society. They see their films as organizing tools for all people engaged in improving our society. Over the years, Newsreel has documented many struggles such as the development and growth of the anti-war movement, the development of the civil rights movement through the black power stage and on into its continuing fight against racism, and the development of the many faceted womans' liberation movement.

They stand in direct opposition to the established media in this country. Their approach to filmmaking is entirely different from the establishments. They feel a definite need and responsibility to become involved in the struggles that they document as well as relying heavily upon the participants in the struggle for the film content. They make no pretext of being "unbiased newspeople"; their films consciously have a biased perspective -- that of the poor, working, black, and Third World People whose struggles and lives we are talking about in the films.

In addition to the films that are made, they distribute films from independen filmmakers and from other countries. Some of the most

■ continued on page 17

Gay Pride March at Fountain Square as people leave for dance Eyephoto: Annice

Gay Pride Weekend

Seventy-five people marched without incident beneath banners proclaiming themselves to be members of the Cincinnati Gay Community, Saturday, April 7. They marched from Washington Park to Fountain Square, escorted by a full complement of Cincinnati police. At the Square speeches and skits were presented to a crowd of about four hundred.

The march was part of the local gay community's a Gay Pride Weekend. Friday night more than eighty people gathered for a gay community dinner at St. John's Unitarian Church. A brunch was held at the church Saturday morning, followed by the march downtown. Saturday evening a dance was held celebrating one year of meeting.

Initial meetings of the Cincinnati Gay Community were held at United Christian Ministries, but soon mo moved to St. John's Unitarian Chu Church, 320 Resor Avenue, in Clifton, where they continue at 7:30 pm Friday nights. The meetings are open to any one.

Free Clinic to Hire M.D.

As we go to press, the Cincinnati Free Clinic is in the process of changing its operations to better serve you. Loss of funding has necessitated cutting administrative expenses. All administrators now make $75.00 a week. Ken Bausch and Beverly Dixon resigned, and an acting director, Barbara Linowitz was hired to work with the one remaining Free Clinic staffer, Ellen Wood.

The board of trustees is negotiating with several doctors to fill the newly established post of medical director.

The Clinic is now open 3:00 to 11:00 pm Monday thru Friday.

The Clinic staff and board hope that hiring a doctor to co-ordinate medical care will provide better quality service and continuity of care for the people who use the clinic. If you have any suggestions for improving the Clinic's services, please call or write the Clinic.
Cincinnati Free Clinic
2444 Vine Street
Cincinnati, Ohio 45219
621-5700

Complete Wounded Knee Coverage – pp. 5-9

2nd Thoughts About Legalization of GRASS – p. 12

Best Buys in Blues Records – p. 16

Straight from the reporting done at Cincinnati Pride on April 7, 1973, in the *Independent Eye*: "Seventy-five people marched without incident beneath banners proclaiming themselves to be members of the Cincinnati Gay Community. They marched from Washington Park to Fountain Square, escorted by a full complement of Cincinnati police. At the Square speeches and skits were presented to a crowd of about 400." Despite press releases and a parade permit, only Channel 9 covered the event and only to show an irreverent skit where characters hit each other. About 150 attendees shared a spaghetti dinner held the night before at St. John's church, and a dinner and dance at the church were held after the march, with an emotional moment featuring Bette Midler's "Friends." The Pride celebration was held one year after the founding of the Cincinnati Gay Community, the first LGBTQ Cincinnati-wide group. (Ohio Lesbian Archives.)

In stark contrast to when Mayor Ted Berry refused to issue a proclamation declaring a "Gay Day" in 1972, Mayor Springer issued a proclamation to declare June 24, 1978, as "Lesbian/Gay Pride Day." This was a bold step for the local government in Cincinnati, as LGBTQ rights ordinances were being repealed or rejected in municipalities all over the country. The proclamation affirmed the right of the LGBTQ community to "inform the public of their concerns and point of view." (Ohio Lesbian Archives.)

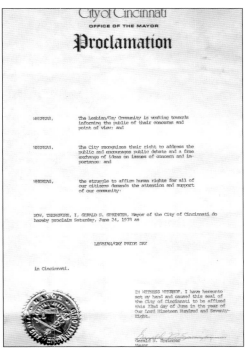

Since 1982, Cincinnatians have annually traveled the 106 northeast miles to participate in Columbus Pride. For some, the event gave them the chance to display their pride in their lives, their unity, and to represent LGBTQ Cincinnati. For others, Columbus Pride provided the opportunity to openly walk down the street holding a partner's hand, something many could not do in Cincinnati for fear that their identity would be revealed to loved ones or employers. (Brian DeWitt.)

Though the spirit of Pride has coursed through the annual celebrations, the actual scenery of Pride has changed several times throughout the years. While the 1973 Pride marched from Washington Park to Fountain Square, the 1985 Pride started at city hall before also ending up at Fountain Square. In 1985, the Pride festival was held behind the Dock, but after concerns were raised that part of that land was city property, the booths were moved to the front of the Dock in 1986. In 2000, Pride began with a rally at Burnet Woods, followed by a parade to Northside and a festival at Hoffner Park. In 2010, the festival moved back to Fountain Square and then on to Sawyer Point in 2012. Indeed, the backdrop has shifted many times, but the foreground of individuals and groups with heads held high can be traced through every route walked by Cincinnati Pride. (Above, Ohio Lesbian Archives; below, Ron Clemons.)

Cincinnati Pride is not only an opportunity for the entire community to come together but also for the community to be led in the parade by Pride marshals—individuals who have displayed extraordinary commitment to amplifying the voice of the Cincinnati LGBTQ community. Past Pride marshals have included longtime activist Shane Que Hee; cofounder of the Ohio Lesbian archives Vic Ramstetter, youth advocate (and first straight ally to be selected) Kathy Laufman, former manager/bartender at the Dock, David Crowley; and tireless promoter Randy Bridges. The roster also features the legendary Peter A. Thompson, whose alter ego Peaches LaVerne was billed as the region's oldest female illusionist. Thompson was the only individual to be elevated to "Queen Mum" after many years serving in the Pride marshal role. (Both, Cheryl Eagleson.)

Before Pride officially kicked off, there first was the annual Pride press conference. Press packets were prepared and sent out to all local media with information on Pride's keynote speaker, the history of the event, and an outline of the festivities. Often, the keynote speaker would say a few words at the press conference, such as Rep. Gerry Studds, the first openly gay member of the US Congress, or prolific author Eric Rofes. Though the room was never filled with to the brim with reporters or cameras, the tradition of the press conference and the commitment to educating the wider public on the importance of Pride far outweighed the number of bodies in the room. (Both, Jeff Bixby.)

Though it is impossible to provide pictures of events that did not happen, some column-width needs to be devoted to the five years that Cincinnati did not have an official Pride parade. From 1996 to 1999, there were festivals, picnics, cruises, and a "Gay Day" at Kings Island amusement park, but Ohioans had to travel to Columbus or Cleveland for their big-city Pride parades. Chris Good, a local pharmacist, told the *Gay People's Chronicle* that the passage of Issue 3 contributed to the parade's demise, saying, "This really seemed to take the wind out of a lot of people's sails." Inspired by Columbus' 1999 Pride, Good, Michael Chanak Jr., and a dedicated committee met monthly at Crazy Ladies Bookstore. In partnership with multiple organizations, they planned a 1.8-mile parade from Burnet Woods Park to Hoffner Park. After a five-year hiatus, Cincinnati Pride returned on June 11, 2000. (Above, Jeff Bixby; below, Michael Chanak Jr.)

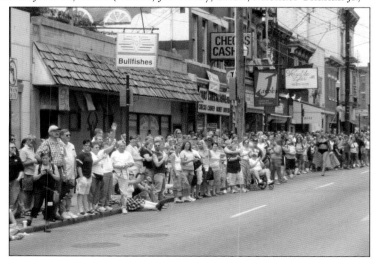

The narrative thread of the "family we choose" has coursed through the history of the LGBTQ community. Though an individual's biological family may distance themselves from their rainbow sheep, the pink wagons of the LGBTQ community have stood at the ready to circle that individual to provide the support and love that may have been lost. Pride annually provides just such an opportunity for that chosen family reunion. But as the years march on and embrace of LGBTQ kin steadily grows, Pride has seen an increase in participation from those biological families that were just not present in past celebrations. From the child raising a sign in support of his same-sex parents, to the straight mothers and fathers walking arm-in-arm with their LGBTQ child, to even organizations that have been formed specifically to bolster LGBTQ family activities, Pride is now a place where all of these clans come together with the singular purpose of lifting each other up, be they families biological or chosen. (Above, Ron Clemons; below, Michael Chanak Jr.)

From the isolated sign holder to the occasional Westboro Baptist Church affiliate, the appearance of some scattered protesters at Cincinnati Pride is as reliable as the rainbow balloons flying above the streets. There has rarely been a time since the LGBTQ community first marched when these protesters have not been wholly outnumbered by celebrants, a ratio that has only become more disparate in numbers as the years march on. Still, these lone wolves continue to show up with their increasingly forlorn signs, providing an annual opportunity for the LGBTQ community to shower them with love in the face of whatever it is the protesters are trying—and failing—to bring to the festivities. (Both, Michael Chanak Jr.)

One of the greatest facets of Pride is the opportunity for individuals to walk behind a banner with an affinity group. Throughout the years, these groups create a community within the larger LGBTQ community, giving people in Cincinnati a sense of place to explore an interest, affiliation, or activity alongside others who share their passion. Pride then lines all these groups up and allows them to proclaim to hordes of witnesses that they are an important piece of the overall LGBTQ kaleidoscope. This visibility certainly enables the group to attract more interested participants. But more importantly, marching also is a highlight for the group itself—a validation that they are doing their part to provide a space where all LGBTQ people are welcome. (Both, Ron Clemons.)

Pride has always been political. Stonewall was political. Fifty years later, the 2019 Pride was political. Heck, the very act of being out of the closet is political. But in recent years, politics has taken root at Pride in much more explicit ways, with candidates actively vying for the LGBTQ vote by having a visible presence during Pride events. Whether it is volunteers from a presidential campaign walking together with their placards aloft or a candidate for local office waving to the crowds by their lonesome, Cincinnati Pride has seen its fair share of myriad candidates working hard to make their case to the assembled masses. Though the candidates have tended to skew Democratic, given the conservative presence nestled within the city, assorted GOP candidates have made their presence known, all hoping secure a few more votes when the next election rolls around. (Both, Michael Chanak Jr.)

From *Moonlight* to *Glee* to *Soap* to *Priscilla, Queen of the Desert*, popular culture has given the LGBTQ community vital representation to see their stories and hear their voices on the screen. These cinematic moments also provide the opportunity for the LGBTQ community to bond over an affinity for the content, a shared point of appreciation that helps to forge new and lasting connections between fans, geeks, nerds, and everyone in between. Whether it is embodying the high-camp content, cross-dressing antics, and a "sweet transvestite from Transylvania" lead of *The Rocky Horror Picture Show* or adding a rainbow twist to the Ohio Garrison of the 501st Legion of the Star Wars costuming club, the pop culture embedded in Pride is most certainly here to stay. (Above, Ron Clemons; below, Michael Chanak Jr.)

What is Pride without drag? Nothing! Okay, well maybe not nothing, but certainly a heck of a lot less entertaining. Whether marching in the parade or wowing the assembled crowds at the festivities, the performance of drag has been embedded in Cincinnati Pride for as far back as anyone can remember. Established performers have led the parade as grand marshals and lip-synched their way across the main stage, but there are also the novices safely trying drag for the first time on the only day of the year when they are surrounded by their LGBTQ siblings. And lest anyone thinks that this is only about drag queens, drag kings have made their mark on Pride with participation and performances that have dazzled all those fortunate enough to have witnessed their talent. (Right, Ty Wesselkamper; below, JAC Stringer.)

Cincinnati native/artist/educator Tim'm West returned to his Ohio roots inspired by the black Pride events in Atlanta, Washington, DC, and the Bay Area. He was determined to create a Cincinnati-based celebration that tapped into one of the largest concentrations of black LGBTQ individuals in the Midwest. The 2018 Cincinnati Black Pride festival featured five days of activities, which included interfaith services, educational events, and the Black Alphabet Film Festival, making Cincinnati only the second city to host the event after Chicago. The theme for the week was "We're Back. We're Black. Get Used To It." The 2019 theme was "We Are Royalty" and featured awards given to elders and youth for their leadership alongside a full roster of events that centered the experience of black LGBTQ people and their role in the movement. (Both, Tim'm West.)

June 21, 2019, was a historic day in Cincinnati as a rainbow Pride flag was raised over city hall for the first time. The decision to fly the flag was unanimously approved by the Cincinnati City Council: Democrats, Republicans, Independents, and Charterites alike. The original rainbow flag was designed by Gilbert Baker for the 1978 San Francisco Gay Freedom Celebration as a symbol under which everyone could assemble, both physically and communally. As Councilwoman Tamaya Dennard said at the Cincinnati ceremony before the rainbow fabric was hoisted aloft, "Today is about saying that we are in this fight for civil rights and social justice and that love is love is love is love." (Right, Ron Clemons; below, David Wolff.)

Take away the rainbow balloons; subtract both the stage and drag artists performing on top of it; and get rid of the vendors, the beer tent, and the free merchandise from the corporate sponsors. What is left are the people, and the people alone will always be enough to constitute Pride in Cincinnati. Over the years, the LGBTQ community in Cincinnati has been through so much: rights granted, rights taken away, celebrations, setbacks, and everything in between. Through it all, LGBTQ Cincinnati neighbors have shown up in force: as individuals expressing their authentic selves and as a community that stands (and marches and dances) stronger together. (Above, Ohio Lesbian Archives; left, Lisa Schreihart.)

About the Ohio Lesbian Archives

The Ohio Lesbian Archives (OLA) was instrumental in providing content for this book. As OLA is already described on page 35, cofounder Phebe Beiser was asked to describe what it is like when she enters the space: "When I walk into the Archives, I am first greeted by a rainbow clock and softball trophy from 1979. Everywhere there are books, file cabinets, and paintings of lesbians. There are few places in the world—nowhere in the region—where I can see myself, my LGBTQ family, and feel so empowered. That is why we continue this work of saving and preserving our stories so we are no longer invisible." For more info, go to ohiolesbianarchives.wordpress.com. (Ohio Lesbian Archives.)

Discover Thousands of Local History Books Featuring Millions of Vintage Images

Arcadia Publishing, the leading local history publisher in the United States, is committed to making history accessible and meaningful through publishing books that celebrate and preserve the heritage of America's people and places.

Find more books like this at
www.arcadiapublishing.com

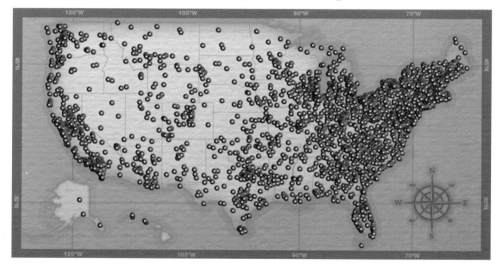

Search for your hometown history, your old stomping grounds, and even your favorite sports team.

Consistent with our mission to preserve history on a local level, this book was printed in South Carolina on American-made paper and manufactured entirely in the United States. Products carrying the accredited Forest Stewardship Council (FSC) label are printed on 100 percent FSC-certified paper.

MADE IN THE USA